SOUL STORIES

SOUL STORIES

AFRICAN AMERICAN CHRISTIAN EDUCATION

REVISED EDITION

ANNE E. STREATY WIMBERLY

Abingdon Press
Nashville

SOUL STORIES
AFRICAN AMERICAN CHRISTIAN EDUCATION (REVISED EDITION)

Copyright © 1994 by Abingdon Press
Revised Edition © 2005 by Abingdon Press

This book is printed on acid-free paper.

Library of Congress Cataloging-in-Publication Data

Wimberly, Anne Streaty, 1936–
    Soul stories: African American Christian education / Anne Streaty Wimberly.—Rev. ed.
        p. cm.
    Includes bibliographical references.
    ISBN 0-687-49432-X (pbk.: alk. paper)
    1. African American Sunday schools. 2. Storytelling in Christian education. 3. Christian education—Biographical methods. 4. African Americans—Religion. I. Title.

BV1523.A37W55 2005
268'.089'96073—dc22

2005003361

All Scripture quotations are taken from the *New Revised Standard Version of the Bible*, copyright © 1989 by the Division of Christian Education of the National Council of the Churches of Christ in the USA. Used by permission.

Quotations by Howard Thurman are from *The Inward Journey*, © 1961 by Howard Thurman, and *Disciplines of the Spirit*, © 1963 by Howard Thurman. Used by permission of Friends United Press.

05 06 07 08 09 10 11 12 13 14—10 9 8 7 6 5 4 3 2 1

MANUFACTURED IN THE UNITED STATES OF AMERICA

To
My husband, Edward Powell Wimberly;
and the memory of my parents,
Valeska Bea Streaty and Robert Harold Streaty, Sr.,
whose attentiveness to story
inspired my own process of story-linking

CONTENTS

ACKNOWLEDGMENTS

Words here seem inadequate to express the depth of my thankfulness for so many who, across the years, have shared their stories with me, invited mine, and in the process taught me the importance and meaning of *soul stories*. My childhood years were enriched by the insistence of my parents, Robert and Valeska Streaty, that being family meant entering daily into times of linking the day's journey, Bible stories, and the inspiring lives of trailblazers of liberation and vocations of hope. This same emphasis on story extended to the church of my childhood, Second Methodist Church, now New Hope United Methodist Church in Anderson, Indiana, where invariably the whole intergenerational family assembled during church school to retell one another the stories and meanings of the day's lessons. Those past years come to me now as magnificent, precious, and unforgettable occasions for which I shall forever remain grateful.

A book could be quickly filled with the names of teachers, friends, relatives, and colleagues across the years whose awareness of the privilege of storytelling and story-listening was demonstrated vividly in their relationships with me and others. Among them are ones whom I feel obliged to mention here: my mentor, caring listener, and supporter, the late Dr. Grant Sneed Shockley; my present story partners including Mrs. Doris Shockley; my sister Mrs. Roberta Streaty Towell; spiritual sisters the Reverend Cecelia Long, Mrs. Pamela Perkins, the Reverend Dr. Carol Helton; the Reverend Tiwirai and Mrs. Adlene Kufarimai and Tatenda, my Zimbabwean family; and my brother in the spirit, Reverend Dr. Michael McQueen; students in my Christian education courses at Interdenominational Theological Center (ITC) in Atlanta, Georgia; the late Bishop L. Scott Allen, Sunday school participants at Rocky Head United Methodist Church in Atlanta, and numerous workshop attendees who gave me opportunity to present the story-linking model and gave encouragement, insight, and affirmation of its usefulness in Christian education;

Dr. Rosemary Keller and Dr. Jack Seymour, who were primary guides in my development of the first edition of *Soul Stories*; and the respondents who gave me the privilege of many, many hours of sharing and the gift of their personal stories.

As with the first edition, this revised edition would not have been possible without the continuing love, counsel, encouragement, and moral support of my husband, Ed. In his writing, too, I have found affirmation of the necessity of recalling our stories and God's Story in our quest as Christians for liberation and hope-building vocation. For his abiding presence and inspiration in my life, I am grateful.

PREFACE

There continues to be a powerful call for Christian education that centers on the stories that frame persons' everyday lives and that bring forth liberating wisdom and hope-building vocation. This call has become even more piercing because of myriad critical issues that are an integral part of current-day stories and due to the diminishing attention to story-sharing in family and community life. The questions ring out: How may our stories connect with God's Story in ways that give liberating wisdom and hope-building vocation along life's sojourn if we do not share them, look at them critically, and discern responsible choices? What may individuals and families learn from sharing stories both of struggle and of promise? This book presents a model of Christian education from an African American perspective that seeks to answer the questions. The model draws on Christian education approaches begun during the slave era and built on the story orientation of African culture.

In this new edition, as in the first, the model focuses on the concept of story-linking. Story-linking is a process whereby Christian education participants connect components of their everyday life stories with the Christian faith story found in Scripture. They also connect their stories with Christian faith heritage stories of African American exemplars, past and present. More specifically, participants link with Bible stories/texts by using them as a mirror through which they reflect critically on the liberation and vocation they are seeking or have already found. The purpose of this linkage is to help persons be aware of the liberating activity of God and God's call to vocation—living in the image of Jesus Christ—in both biblical and present times.

In linking with Christian faith heritage stories of African Americans, Christian education participants relate themselves to exemplars who chose ways of living in community that were informed by the gospel. The intent is for African Americans to be encouraged and inspired by the lives of people who faced life circumstances with which they can readily identify. And, it is aimed toward participants' choosing to cooperate with this activity by acting in ways that are liberating for them and others.

Five primary assumptions undergird the story-linking process found in the early slave community:

1. Christian education can be strengthened or extended beyond the present paradigm by reclaiming the story-linking process found in the early slave community.
2. The story-linking model is appropriately undertaken in intergenerational Christian education settings.
3. There is similarity between the issues as well as the contexts that are addressed in Scripture and the issues and the contexts African Americans address today.
4. The story-linking model can be used appropriately in traditional Christian education settings such as the church school, Bible study groups, retreats, and in combinations of age-/stage groups. It is also useful in the home and other community locations.
5. The story-linking model holds importance for Christian education leaders, teachers, and participants alike.

Impetus for Writing This Book

Soul Stories has emerged out of my recognition that Christian education for African Americans continues to face significant challenges. On the one hand, its historical role in African American churches is undisputed. Leaders see clearly the potential of intentionally planned educational experiences as well as worship for providing approaches, direction, and resources that meet current challenges of African Americans. Because of their view of the pivotal role of Christian education, some churches have given specific attention to redesigning or appending the more traditional-oriented planned programs.

On the other hand, there continues to be much discussion among present and future African American church leaders about the great challenge currently facing Christian education in African American churches and communities. Many churches are paying more attention to worship and giving less attention to planned forms of Christian education beyond the worshiping congregation, often because they do not see the relationship between dwindling numbers and approaches deemed irrelevant. In far too many instances, intentionally planned Christian education programs are neglected in African American church life.

Agreement exists among African American Christian educators and leaders about the search of individuals and families for greater relevance and effectiveness in Christian educational contexts and processes. People desire a context and a process for exploring, reflecting on, and deciding on ways of living as Christians. There is need for reflection on who we are, how we are living in community, the choices we have made, and the purpose we see for our lives in the face of our everyday life experiences and the predictable life crises we undergo.

Individuals and families are searching for forums in which they can address who they are and can become in the fray of life's realities. They also desire guidance in seeing options and deciding, consciously and intentionally, on wise ways of living and serving as Christians that are liberating for them and others and that imbue their ongoing life sojourn with a hopeful purpose. This means that persons are seeking help with the task of ethical decision making. It is out of my recognition of these needs and desires in African American congregations that this book is written.

How This Second Edition Differs from the First

This second edition differs from the earlier edition in two primary ways. First, I have inserted wisdom as a significant aspect of the liberation-directed story-linking process, and hope as a necessary part of the emphasis on vocation. My use of wisdom builds on the idea set forth in the book *In Search of Wisdom*, edited by me with coeditor Evelyn Parker, which highlights the increasing fervent cry of persons for wisdom in what is being termed a nihilistic age where wisdom somehow seems to be in short supply.[1] My use of hope also reflects not simply persons' yearning for a wise life perspective centered on integrity, courage, and faith in God needed to conduct their lives in turbulent times, but the need for individual and collective effort to shape our world toward hopeful ends.

Second, in the first edition, the story-linking process included case studies of individuals whose personal experiences both mirrored the unique needs of persons in the African American community and offered a means of facilitating group story-sharing and reflection. The stories necessarily drew attention to individuals' relationships in family and community. However, the focus of the stories on individuals reflected the angst among African Americans at that time about claiming positive identity given by God, and individual strengths needed for Christian living and vocation under continuing difficult circumstances of being black in the United States. The emphasis also opened the way for persons to grapple with dominant society issues related to meanings of and threats to self-fulfillment. It is fair to say, though, that this focus emphasized the all too prevalent individualistic value orientation of Western society at a time when family issues were coming to the forefront. As a result, the issues of families that were imbedded in the individuals' stories were not highlighted to any great degree.

This second edition responds to the need for new concentration on the African American family and, therefore, presents family-focused case studies. The introduction of family stories reflects my recognition that many families are struggling with a real collapse of the kind of close-knit relationships and "village life" found in earlier periods of African American history. This recognition is also supported by religionists and community leaders who describe a present requirement for emphasis on family. There is need for immediate or "up-close" families and the extended "village" family to embrace, model, and convey meanings of both liberating wisdom and hope-building purpose in the present era of rootlessness, lovelessness, hopelessness, and spiritual impoverishment.[2]

Implicit in the family orientation is my awareness that the experiences of persons are informed by the system of beliefs and values expressed in family settings. There is a profound connection between what is going on in families and what happens in the lives of individuals. Thus, when we engage the stories of families, we gain insights not simply on family dynamics but on the journey of individuals. The inclusion of family stories in this edition is intended to invite reflection on this organic function of the family context in promoting and sustaining liberating wisdom and hope-building vocation. Also, because the congregation is an important extended family or "village" of fictive kin—not blood relatives—who carry out a mediating role in the formation of wise life perspectives, some attention is given in the story-linking process in this volume to this larger family.[3] In short, this edition of *Soul Stories* gives pivotal attention to stories of families.

Prologue: The Quest for Liberation and Hope-Building Vocation

We may not live out all our days
Tensing every nerve to do our best
To find at last a dead goal, a false road.
How may we know?
Is there no guide for us?
No shining light by which our steps are led?
Through all the chaos of our years
We seek to know.

—Howard Thurman
The Inward Journey

Christian education that is relevant in and beyond the present era must help us to grapple with the realities of our everyday lives and to envision how we as Christians can go forward in liberating and hopeful ways. This view of the purpose of Christian education has become a dominant and repetitive response of African American Christians to whom I have posed the question: What is most needed in Christian education today and tomorrow? A principal response also comes forward to the question: How should we carry out Christian education that addresses this purpose?

Repeatedly, I have heard persons describe their intense search for opportunities to tell and receive direction for the stories that frame their existence. From their perspective, relevant approaches to Christian education free us *from* what they describe as experiences of "zones of incomplete communication" *to* engagements in direct person-to-person, face-to-face story-sharing. The need for this kind of aliveness is particularly important because of the way we live in our busy, fast-paced, techno-centered world. Life tends to move forward with ever-increasing reliance on interactions via machines and a depleting store of trust, connectedness in family, and sense of community.[1]

One participant in a conversation made the comment: "We have come to rely on cell phones, voice mail, e-mail, the Internet, and other kinds of 'distance' communicating. Our connecting in this way is simply the way it is, and I'm not adverse to it. It has advantages. But, we are craving up-close 'in the flesh' telling and listening partners. We aren't finding them in our families at home. We are missing them in our communities where neighbors don't know, trust, or speak with one another. There is no substitute for up-close relating; and that kind of relating is what Christian education ought to be about."[2] These comments about "distant" communication mirror, in fact, a growing concern that "as people become more entrenched in this communicative style, the danger is that they will invest less energy and expect less of themselves in traditional face-to-face relationships. And, the less people give of themselves in these relationships, the hungrier they and the people in their lives are apt to become for a caring, in-person listening presence."[3]

The key point here is that we learn and mature as persons, and grasp meanings of liberation and our vocation or purpose in life in caring, face-to-face human relationships in family and community. Caring relationships refer to persons' affirmation of one another, availability and intentionality in story-sharing, and show of concern for one another's well-being in the throes of life's sojourn. As part of the community, the church is the extended family and must give attention to these relationships. The task of Christian education in our churches is to create opportunities that help to ground persons in these relationships. By doing so, we help to lay the ground for liberation and vocation. We foster hope.

In conversations about Christian education, African Americans also continue to highlight the key role of Scripture. They want to enter it with their stories and questions and discern what it has to say to the very lives we live and hope for. The engagement of Scripture is needed to guide us. Of pivotal importance, too, are the stories of those who have been able to surmount the storms of life and carry out hope-building vocations. We recognize that we are not in touch with the kinds of stories used by our forebears to find meaning and convincing reason to continue in spite of life's absurdities; and we are searching for and need the wisdom of exemplars to enrich and inspire us in an age of dwindling cultural resources.[4] Christian education is needed to help us reconstruct the cultural resources we so sorely need now and in the foreseeable future.

What clearly emerges in conversations with African Americans is the role of Christian education in honoring persons' quest for the soul's story to be shared and for a larger story—God's Story—to inform and transform that story. Persons are in pursuit of liberation and hope-building vocation, or a way of being and acting in life that grants them a sense of positive relatedness to God, self, others, and all things. "Our need," they say, "is for a Christian education context and a process that helps us to discern hopeful reasons to keep on keeping on. We want to get in touch with the 'more' in life."

The Power of Story and Storytelling

The quest for story and storytelling to bring relevance to Christian education is not surprising. Story is a powerful part of human existence. We humans live an evolving narrative, or story, that forms from the storied world around us. Life as a story is eventful. It is not static. Our lives have a past, a present, and a future in some place and in some circumstance. Our lives move on. Or, it can be said that human experiences take on a narrative quality as they unfold within the framework of context, time, and space.[5]

Those who emphasize the importance of a story orientation also tell us that we humans think in narrative form and that our communicative process is inherently narrative. For example, Theodore Sarbin, a narrative theorist, says that we humans think, perceive, image, make moral choices, and engage in discourse according to a narrative structure.[6] Donald Capps, pastoral theologian, reminds us that we have the capacity to reflect on our lived stories.[7] Andrew Lester, also a pastoral theologian, adds that this reflection helps us to see alternative directions in our lives and our reframing our stories according to the convictions and values we hold. We not only participate in constructing our stories but also in revising them throughout our lives.[8]

Religious educator Thomas Groome states that to be a person is to live in a story; and sharing our stories helps us appreciate ourselves as agent-subjects in history. By sharing, we recognize and communicate the resources and wisdom contained in our stories. Moreover, says Jerry Stone, story-sharing provides an approach to Christian education "that helps to heal a paralysis of the mind if not always of the body."[9] Building on the work of Gabriel Fackre, Stone highlights not simply the healing properties of story-sharing, but the potential there exists for exploring how the *canonical story* or the canon of biblical literature, the *life story*, and the unfolding *communal story* relate. Stone adds to this the richness of vision that can be gained from the biographies or life stories of persons in or near our present communities "whose lives embody the convictions of our community."[10] Peter Gilmour, also a Christian educator, stresses that our stories are the "sacred texts" of our lives that open the way for transformation when we tend to our memoirs. Through remembering the "sacred texts" of our lives, we come in contact with the wisdom inherent in them and with the Holy One, the Source of hope and healing.[11]

Storytelling is not new. Across generations and cultures, storytelling has been an integral part of life. The stories people told revealed the roots of their histories, aspects of the lives they lived in the present, and the lives they imagined and hoped for in the future.[12] Moreover, there is a narrative structure of the Bible that unfolds in telling the Story of God and the importance of that Story in shaping the character of people's lives.[13] In fact, our African American forebears in slavery were cognizant of the Bible as a storied document with which they could link their own stories, and from which they could find direction and hope in the hard trials and tribulations of their circumstances. Their storytelling continued a revered African ancestral manner of relating in community. It allowed them to reveal the depth of their own experiences and pose tough questions about life. It connected them to God's guiding, sustaining, and transforming Story in the Bible, to resources from the past, and led them to decide how they would act amid the realities of life as moral and accountable beings.[14]

Consequently, we can say that over generations and cultures, including in Bible times, people have been a storied people. The ongoing call for story and storytelling in Christian education is, thus, a plea for us to recover the central role of story and storytelling for the liberating wisdom and hope-building vocation.

Reflection Exercise

Consider your own experiences as a leader, teacher, or participant in Christian education. In what settings have you participated? What prompted your involvement as a leader, teacher, or participant? What did you hope would happen in your life and in the lives of others as the result of your role?

The Importance of Liberation and Liberating Wisdom in Story-Sharing

Liberation has punctuated the story of African Americans beginning with the sojourn of our forebears in slavery. It became encapsulated in the prophetic statement: "God wants us free!" which voiced the belief in God's desire for our freedom from humiliation and subjugation to live and move and have our being with human dignity in a just society. It became the centerpiece of a black liberation theology that gave priority to the theological and ethical position that not simply does God want us free, but God through Jesus Christ sides with oppressed people in their struggle for freedom.[15] Clearly, this struggle has become ongoing. It seems to confront each new generation with renewed responsibility.[16] At the same time, the failure of past efforts to change the world has resulted in the conclusion by some that "the high moment of liberation theology has passed."[17]

However, I have learned from African Americans in our churches, communities, and seminary classes that we cannot tarry on the issue of the current efficacy of liberation theology fashioned in and developed further after the mid-twentieth-century Civil Rights Movement. Indeed, two key approaches to liberation have surfaced in these conversations. First, it is essential that we rearticulate what we understand liberation to be from inside the stories of our lives. Second, we must search for the wisdom necessary for us to freely decide a way forward with God *anyhow*, based on our knowing God's hope in us and our hope in God.

A View of Liberation from the Inside

As we moved toward the end of the twentieth century, I asked persons to describe what it means to be liberated. I received from them immensely varied but interconnected responses, which I shared in the first edition of *Soul Stories*. When I asked new groups of respondents to compare those descriptions to ones they would give today, they readily affirmed the views and the situation out of which the views came as currently applicable. They resonated with the following perspective given by an African American male; and, though their situations differed in content, the story still contained themes that spoke volumes not simply about their individual lives but about family stories.

"When I think about liberation, what comes to my mind, first, is a feeling of being all right inside myself. I feel like it's okay to be me because I count in God's eyes. I can also be myself because I know I'm all right as a person, and I'm respected for who I am. But, then, sometimes other folk don't think I'm all right. It seems like they don't want to let me go on with my life in the same way they are allowed to. That's when me and God have to talk, 'cause the way I think God sees me and the way others do are just not the same. You know what I mean?

"Like, on my job, I feel like I can't advance because of who I am as a black man. The attitudes they show toward me as a black man aren't that good either. That's wrong. Well, because I can't seem to advance, I can't get for me and my family all the things we really need. There are times when we see our way clear and we get caught up with things like medical bills and clothes for the kids.

"Well, about liberation? I know what it's not. And, I know that sometimes you see it, sometimes you don't. I know my children see what's going on. I wonder sometimes what it is doing to them. But I do the best I can, and me and my wife keep on trying to encourage our children. We keep our hopes up. So far they're doing well, where some other kids aren't. You know what no hope can do. Whenever I can, I try to do whatever I can for the kids in the neighborhood. People don't always think that black men care, but I do. No, I don't have all the answers for them or me. I can use some help. Like I said, I do the best I can, but sometimes I know that's not good enough.

"All in all, I'm blessed in so many ways. I was able to get an education. Now, I didn't get to go to college, but I did get vocational technical training, and I took opportunities that came my way to upgrade my skills. That's a part of being liberated too. I want more for my children. Sure, it can be hard to get an education. But then you have to want to get it, and it helps when somebody's there to encourage you. It is something that, when you get it, nobody can take it away from you.

"Well, let me say one more thing. At one time in my life, I know I wasn't going in the right direction. I wasn't spiritually right or men-

liberation

tally right and I guess you might say any other kind of right. Things have changed as far as that's concerned. Somewhere along the line, I got a whole new lease on life. I feel like it was the power of God that helped me to turn my life around. I feel all right in my soul, and I try to do what's right by others. To me, that's liberation too. Then, too, my family is my pride and joy. There's nobody that keeps us from loving one another. Then, too, there's nobody that keeps us from helping others that aren't close family. Like education, nobody can take that away either. And isn't that what being a Christian is all about? Liberation? There are so many things to it. It's not just one thing."

Of course the details of others' stories differ from the one told above in accordance with the particular context and nature of the struggles, concerns, hopes, and desires of individuals and family members. Stories tell of divorce, remarriage, and blended families in an age of few long-term marriages, the journey of single adults, grandparents raising grandchildren, varied circumstances of senior adults, and responsibilities of family members for the eldest among us. Still other stories center on family crises—situations of economic need, incarceration, addictions, critical illness, and experiences of bereavement—while others include joys and celebration in times of blessing and accomplishment.

The complexities of our time are also etched in stories mirroring the increasing multicultural landscape of the country and African Americans' experiences of racial inequities and maltreatment amid new socio-relational dynamics. And, fresh challenges appear in the stories of Christian families whose young find affinity with Islam and discontent with Christianity in general and black Christianity in particular.

Regardless of story, the theme of liberation sought or found often surfaces as persons disclose the details of their journeys, raise questions, and offer commentaries on what is going on in their individual and family lives. The quest for liberation comes through questions like: "How is it possible for my family to get free from the situation we are in?" "What do I need to do to arrive at a breakthrough with my teenage child?" "What, really, does it mean to be African American and free in this present age?" Or the liberation quest emerges in comments such as: "The way things are now on my job, I feel like I've hit a dead end," or "I'm boxed in." "There are so many things going on, it just seems like I'm going in circles and can't find a way out." "We, as a people, are not free as long as we are racially profiled, live in environmentally unsafe places, and continue to confront unequal life chances in the workplace, education, health services, and criminal justice system."

Evidence of liberation found by persons is also noted in comments like the following: "I never thought we'd get to this point. Our family has been through a lot. But, we've come out on the other side of darkness into the light of day. The death of a child is not easy. But we know we're going to be all right." "Whatever comes, I know God, on whom I can count to give me the freedom and determination I need to carry on. Really, I'm free to cry out to God knowing God hears me. And, even though the answers I want don't always come, or don't come when I want them, I get an answer nonetheless; and that's all right. The God I know frees me to keep on keeping on when all else fails and it seems like I'm hemmed in on every side. It's like the Bible says, 'Surely I know the plans I have for you, says the LORD, plans for your welfare and not for harm, to give you a future with hope' [Jeremiah 29:11]."

Overall, however, African Americans today tend to agree with the closing question and comment appearing at the end of the earlier cited African American male's story: "Liberation? There are so many things to it. It's not just one thing." It continues to be the case today that liberation is not a singular or onetime accomplishment. Rather it appears to be a multidimensional process that doesn't stop. Moreover, the various facets are intricately interwoven. That is, persons assign causal relationships to the various facets of liberation. They will say, for example, that they or their families cannot be liberated in this way because they are not free in that way.

Others say that one dimension of liberation or another is attained at a particular point in life while other dimensions remain elusive. Or, some dimensions are maintained over long periods while others seem to be short-lived. Yet, what has also emerged in conversations is that a living faith in God through Jesus Christ makes a difference in how we look at, live, and care for every other dimension of liberation. This aliveness happens for some of us through an extraordinary experience of God's presence or activity in our lives. For others, it comes through a gradual awakening of God as the Source of our experiences of liberation that deepens as we link our stories with Scripture and become privy to stories of God's activity in the lives of others. A living faith anchors us in the larger Story of God, which gives us a unique and empowering sense of freedom in the midst of the "stuff" of life that might otherwise "hem us in." For this reason, the following seven dimensions of liberation highlighted by my conversation partners begin with spiritual liberation.

DIMENSION ONE: SPIRITUAL LIBERATION. Liberation results when we choose to link our lives with God's Story revealed in the person of Jesus Christ and know ourselves as called to make that Story come alive in our lives. We see the difference between living that doesn't work for us and life in positive relation to God, self, others, and all things. We allow the Story of God and the good news of Jesus Christ to direct our lives. This is liberation through religious transformation. As a result of this transformation, we enter into a relationship with God and act on our knowing ourselves as called to be disciples of Jesus Christ in ways that free us *from* acquiescence *to* a dead-end or "boxed-in" existence *to* our embrace of and acting on God's hope and purpose for our lives. The African American man quoted earlier does not engage in a lot of God-talk. However, he is clear that it was by the power of God that his life was turned in the right direction. After this point, he resolves to live the right way by doing right by others.

DIMENSION TWO: ETHICAL LIBERATION. The second dimension of liberation involves our embrace of and living according to a values framework centered on our knowing all of life comprising the whole inhabited world or *oikoumene*—humankind and otherkind—as gift. From a Christian perspective, we acknowledge ourselves and other human beings as valued beings created by God and for whom Jesus came as *Emmanuel*— God with us. We see our identity and the identities of others through the eyes of God and our responsibility to act on this understanding of giftedness and value. We also see the interrelatedness of humans with all that comprises the earth community as God's created order; and we acknowledge and accept our responsibility to care for the whole environment and to assure environmental safety and justice in and beyond our communities. In this kind of liberation, we are freed *from* humans'—our own—tendencies to name and foster an existence and relationships that harm the lives of human beings and otherkind *to* form, hold to, and act on a framework of values that contribute to building up and nurturing all of life. Although the African American man whose story appeared earlier did not refer to an environmental ethics or care for the whole of God's creation, a values orientation focused on doing "right by others" and showing love is clearly present.

DIMENSION THREE: MATERIAL LIBERATION. To be liberated is to have the wherewithal by which to receive and maintain, at minimum, the basic necessities of life. From the Christian perspective, this third dimension of liberation refers to assuring that all God's children have adequate material supports such as housing, economic means, food, and clothing to survive and thrive with human dignity and respect. This is liberation *from* material need *to* material sustenance. In the African American man's story, note this liberation was elusive for him. In his case, as in the case of poor people, blocks hinder the attainment of what is fully needed for this to occur.

DIMENSION FOUR: SOCIOPOLITICAL LIBERATION. A fourth dimension of liberation is closely aligned to the third. It is to be equal participants in policy-making on and beneficiaries of the political, occupational, educational, residential, health-care, and recreational systems comprising the civic life of the community and nation. For Christians, this means assuring the necessities of every member of God's household through not only granting our full participation in civic life, but also our taking seriously our civic duty. This is liberation *from* human disenfranchisement *to* human enfranchisement.

DIMENSION FIVE: PSYCHOSOCIAL LIBERATION. Liberation is the experience of individuals and family members not simply of respectful and affirming treatment by others with whom we relate, but of our knowing ourselves as valuable creations of God even in the face of disaffirmation. We are not shackled by how society or anyone else sees us, and we seek to address denigrating or abusive treatment. From the Christian perspective, attaining this form of liberation requires recognition and willingness to confront within ourselves and in the immediate and wider relational contexts blocks or hindrances to positive regard for ourselves. This extends to blocks to positive regard for our ethnicity and culture. We may refer to this activity as liberation *from* denigration and dehumanization *to* positive self-valuing of who and Whose we are as individuals, families, and ethnic cultural group. The man in the story was ill-treated at work, but he received the kind of love at home that made a difference in his life. However, in some stories, the experience of maltreatment at work and in other sectors of society at large, as well as abusive relationships in the family or violence in community settings, belies persons' experience of psychosocial liberation.

DIMENSION SIX: EDUCATIONAL LIBERATION. Liberated persons can see possibilities of breaking out of narrow boundaries of thought, knowledge, feelings, and limited beliefs in the self's ability to act. This is liberation *from* miseducation, no education, and no vision. It is liberation *to* active learning and arriving at a vision for living. For Christians, it entails active engagement in Christian teaching and learning and arriving at a vision of our lives as Christians. Note in the man's story that he saw ways of doing what he could in the best way he could in spite of adversity. He encouraged his children and maintained hope, and he believed that encouragement, hope, and doing his best made a difference.

DIMENSION SEVEN: COMMUNAL LIBERATION. When we are liberated, we recognize our need to share ourselves and our stories with another. We also recognize our need to receive the same from others. From the Christian perspective, we see life as a gift worthy of sharing. This is liberation *from* our self's adoption of a stance of isolation or of being set outside community *to* a commitment to be in significant relationship with those in our family and non-kin circles as a caring, sharing, and listening presence. The nature of this dimension of liberation appears in the earlier mentioned story of the African American man. In that story, he made reference to doing whatever he could for others in the neighborhood and of helping others not simply in but beyond his immediate family.

Liberation that frees us to be *in* community includes a second aspect. We are never fully liberated until we become aware of others' need for liberation and accept as obligatory our responsibility for contributing to the liberation of others. This aspect of communal liberation entails mutual caring, or the movement *away from* concerns and actions aimed only toward the self and *toward* actions with and on behalf of others in the way Jesus did. Again, in the case of the earlier mentioned story, the African American man was aware of the needs of others and sought to provide for them in a way that they could experience it. In our communities today, this kind of liberation would become recognized in caring for the least among us—the imprisoned, the homeless, the elderly, the sick, the abused.

We need to be aware, however, that just as people express what liberation means, they also have perceptions and experiences of what it means to fall short of it. The African American man's experience and perception of "falling short" prompted his statement that he did not have all the answers. Thus, the quest for liberation and the need for direction in finding pathways to it continued.

Reflection Exercise

As leaders, teachers, and participants in Christian education, you may see yourselves in the questions and comments on liberation appearing earlier in this section on liberation. And, you may see yourselves in the African American man's story. Conversely, your questions, comments, and story, as well as your particular life circumstances, may differ from these. What questions would you raise about your own liberation? What comments would you make about your own liberation? How is your story like or different from the story of the African American man? Your views of liberation may also be similar or dissimilar to the seven dimensions of liberation outlined above. In what ways have you experienced the dimensions of liberation outlined above? What blocks to the various aspects of liberation have you experienced?

The Importance of Wisdom

The liberation on which African Americans continue to focus is multidimensional and holistic. Sustaining a journey that can bring forth our experience of this kind of liberation requires what my conversation partners describe as unyielding tenacity and a wise manner of being, thinking, and behaving in the world. We need a liberating wisdom, they say—a wisdom that frees within us the essential integrity and courage needed for us to form wholeness-producing life perspectives, as well as to make choices and take actions resulting in holistic liberation. In the book *In Search of Wisdom: Faith Formation in the Black Church*, I say that this kind of wisdom comes from relating to the One in whom we anchor our lives. Specifically, "it relies on our faith in God, openness to God and discernment of God's desire for our lives."[18] An example of this kind of reliance appears in the earlier mentioned comment of one of my conversation partners who experienced God's promise declared in Jeremiah 29:11.

As Christians, we also form liberating wisdom from our knowing Jesus Christ and his example after which we are to pattern our lives. Indeed, the African American male's story of service in community after the model of Jesus tells us that liberating wisdom coming from knowing Jesus results in our choosing a life direction that points toward what is good and just—toward wholeness for ourselves and our communities.

It is important to say, too, that just as holistic liberation is not easily attained or maintained, so also we may struggle to grasp liberating wisdom. Yet, liberating wisdom is also understood as a kind of knowing that "allows freedom to doubt, question, lament life's realities, and to unlearn and relearn meanings of faith throughout life."[19] Liberating wisdom is expressed through our acknowledging these very real attributes of our human nature and our openness to disclosing them in times of story-sharing. Christian education that invites us into story-sharing is ministry that recognizes us as wisdom seekers whose quest is to reflect honestly on the details of our lives, on forms of liberation gained and not yet realized, and on a way forward with God.

A View of Hope-Filled Vocation

Vocation is not unrelated to liberation and liberating wisdom. When we see a purpose for our lives that is related to caring for and helping others, we have grasped a liberating wisdom that, in turn, liberates us to be in vocation. Yet, in this current era, there are constricted views of what *vocation* means to Christians. This situation carries over from the time of the first edition of *Soul Stories*.

A part of the present condition relates to the particularized journey of African Americans in the larger commodified culture where human worth is determined by what and how much we make and own. In this situation, the human quest for a sense of value and belonging based on the acquisition of "things" results in efforts to get those things. In commenting about this situation, one person said: "Just look at the media. It bombards us with goods to buy. We begin to think we *must* have this or that and, therefore, we look at it as stuff we just can't do without. And, doesn't it become a matter of keeping up with the Joneses? I think so!" Another commented: "When so much emphasis and energy are placed on getting whatever we can for ourselves, even though we know there are things we need to survive, we lose sight of what we ought to be doing to make a better world." Discussions about the meaning of vocation also invariably trigger memories of news reports of heads of corporations and others in power in wider society whose clamber for greater and greater economic gain and power belies an understanding of vocation or service on behalf of a better world.

At the same time, although my conversation partners heartily agreed on the realities of commodified culture and on the strictures it places on a vocational orientation, they were adamant that a sense of vocation has not been entirely lost among us. In particular, participants in one of my seminary classes told of their own calls to Christian vocation, their present participation in it, and of others they know who are living it. We also recalled together the numerous action stories of Christian vocation appearing in the remarkable volume of research by Andrew Billingsley entitled *Mighty Like a River*.[20] Nonetheless, there was unanimity in the belief that urgent attention is still needed to the importance of renewed focus on Christian vocation that builds hope in an age when far too many are hopeless. One person's perspective was that "we need to keep looking at what it means to be in Christian vocation; and, we need to look closely at how it can be hope-building." The expressions of persons contained in the first edition of *Soul Stories* became a basis for discussion and the sharing of similar views. But, meanings of hope-filled vocation brought new insights.

Continuing Views of Christian Vocation

"Vocation is what you do for others, whether you get paid for it or not. It can be related to your occupation, but it doesn't have to be. But the main thing is that you do it because God called you to do it." This statement originally came from a church school class participant some years ago. However, it still has salience today, along with the words of another class member that "as Christians, we know within ourselves that God wants us to carry out our lives in a way that we and others are built up."

The central idea of vocation as calling continues in the conversation of persons today. For some, an initial impression of a direction toward a specific vocation came at an early time in their lives. But they did not fully understand it as God's call. Even when God's call is fully comprehended, persons sometimes say no to it, either because they don't perceive it as possible or because of other internal or external blocks. Others became aware of their call to vocation when they were "pressed into" a particular helping role or when someone else identified gifts they had that could be used to benefit the community. Still others observed in the lives of acquaintances and in their own that the call to vocation can change at different points in one's unfolding life story. However, there was agreement that whatever direction it takes at whatever point in time, the call to vocation is for as long as we are able to carry it out. A key view is:

"If vocation is what you do for others, whether you get paid for it or not, then age doesn't matter. Take, for example, volunteering. That can be done at any age. Take, for example, my elderly neighbor. She is raising one of her grandchildren. She is giving that child a stable home that isn't possible with the parents. I'd say she's in vocation, and she's certainly not getting paid for it, not that she shouldn't get paid."

At the same time, African Americans continue to be very aware that when they are called to occupation-related vocations, there is need for preparation, and that is where their calling can still be blocked. Consider the following story:

"I always wanted to be somebody and do something important with my life. I'm not sure where I got the idea, but I wanted to be a doctor. When I was a kid, I used to dream about it. I used to ask for a play doctor's bag for Christmas. The only thing was, whenever I said anything about it, I was laughed at. I was told, 'How do you think you're going to do that? Don't you know you're black, boy? There's nobody out there who wants you to get anywhere, and who's going to see that you get anywhere?' They would say, 'Just look where we live. People have a hard time leaving this place.' You see, we lived in the projects. The teachers in school also treated us as though we weren't supposed to go anywhere either. Somewhere along the line, I stopped believing in me and my dream. That dream got shattered.

"Well, I didn't become the doctor I wanted to be, although I have a good friend who grew up in my neighborhood who beat the odds and did become one. I had some bad times and got into some trouble along the way. But there was somebody looking after me. I guess you'd say I had an angel watching after me. I was able to put my life together, and I am doing something important with my life. I did get through high school. I got involved in a church through a man who witnessed to me about God on a job I took after graduation. I guess you'd call it a miracle.

"It took me a while, but I decided I wanted to help other kids get out of where somebody told me I couldn't. God helped me to see that I had to do this. I guess you'd say God called me. And, when I realized I had to do something like this, I kept on 'til I found a way of doing it. Now, I am directing a community youth program, and I am going to college to become a guidance counselor. I'm in a place where

I can tell the youth that they can go beyond the limits others set for us and that God wants that for us. I just hope I can help them see that and can move some stumbling blocks along the way."

Connecting Liberating Wisdom and Hope-Building Vocation

The African American's story presented above is an important one because it not only gives us a perspective on the meaning of vocation, but also the connection between liberating wisdom and the embrace of hope-building vocation. The young man had an early sense of life direction. But, he did not have the opportunity to discover whether this impression was a definitive call from God. Because he bought into the limits set by others, his response to it was stifled. His liberation to pursue the occupation-focused vocation of physician was blocked by negative regard from others and negative self-regard. However, the young man later received a definitive call from God and responded to it. He identified it as coming through God's help. He formed a liberating wisdom that became concrete in his recognition of God's call to him; and he acknowledged God's help that moved him to act. The liberating wisdom he formed was an attitudinal frame that made possible his acceptance of the guidance of a caring other he saw as an angel who watched after him.

Wisdom freed him *from* the shackles of negative self-regard based on others' assessment of him. It freed him *to* see and choose a hope-filled vocation in which he became instrumental in others' liberation. The unfolding of liberating wisdom into hope-filled vocation in his story is akin to what the famous African American forebear and exemplar of the faith Frederick Douglass wrote about in his memoir. Douglass described freedom as an experience that sharpens moral and mental vision[21] and brings forth a willingness to bear the responsibilities of being a free agent.[22] And, responsibility-taking entails persons' acting zealously as protectors of one another.[23] They engage in service on behalf of others not because it is either popular or reputable, but rather because of the wish to learn and to delight the soul by doing all that enhances the condition of others.[24] The task of Christian education is to engage persons in storytelling as a means of inspiring their movement toward this kind of engagement. As one conversation partner put it:

"We know from the Bible that it's possible to make it in hard trials, and that's what much of life is. We also know that our African American forebears made it. We seem to forget that. We need to remember. We need to build strength from the resources from the past and know that the resources here in the present are looking right at us. We just have to see them."

It is the case that not everyone comes to Christian education with notions of what the word *vocation* means. Often, it is in dialogue and storytelling that the meaning takes shape. Moreover, the meaning may begin to become personalized only when helpful questions are asked, such as:

- What are you doing with your life as a Christian?
- What is God calling you to be and do?
- What meaning and purpose do you assign to your life as a Christian?

Questions such as these tend to open a new window of thought and to give persons an opportunity to voice their experiences and their perceptions of vocation.

New Insights About Hope-Building Vocation

I have discovered that persons continue to develop understandings of Christian vocation when they see how it is carried out in Bible stories and everyday life. Indeed, they internalize meanings of hope-building vocation from their linking with Scripture and from what they see and hear from Christian exemplars. This is true for adults; but, it is especially the case with the young. Youth participants in the Youth Hope-Builders Academy of Interdenominational Theological Center in Atlanta, Georgia, want to know how and why adults got involved in what they are doing and what it means to them. They also grapple with what hope there is for their life direction when adult Christians fail to carry out in their lives the kind of vocation they talk to youth about. Our youth are searching for guidance in making sense out of life. They question God. They struggle with their identities, their social contexts, their relationships, and the things that happen to them. They want and need encouragement, affirmation, and support in their quest for liberating wisdom and at least some notions if not a clear picture of what hope-building vocation means for their lives.

Of course African American adults, as well, want to know how Scripture "speaks" a hopeful word to them; and they observe the lives of persons around them and go through questioning similar to our youths. They, too, need encouragement, affirmation, and support. Both want and need opportunities to consider what is going on in their lives, to affirm the positives, and to find how to address precisely the negatives.

The Challenge Restated: Responding to the Soul's Yearning for Liberation and Vocation

Christian educators in African American settings are challenged to provide a Christian education for liberation and vocation. This involves both the *content,* or basic meanings of liberation and vocation from an African American Christian perspective, and a culturally sensitive *process.* The basic content builds upon the expressions of liberation and vocation from personal experiences such as those related earlier in this chapter. It is rooted in the desire of African Americans for hope and wholeness, a hunger to move beyond external and internal barriers that block experiences of positive relationships with God, self, others, and all things. I also understand the basic content to be built on the view of vocation as African Americans' desire to see and act on our value, and to decide how we will carry out a hope-building purpose in the world as human beings who are Christian.

A culturally sensitive process will enable persons to break the silences into which we have often been relegated. The challenge is to give persons voice—to offer a caring place for the sharing of stories and the opportunity to envision a future of hope. I have identified this process as story-linking. The chapters that follow are designed to invite us into this process of sharing.

Chapter 1 presents the story-linking process in detail. The chapter describes the key aspects of the process with focus on engaging the everyday story, engaging the Christian faith story in the Bible, engaging Christian faith stories from the African American heritage, and engaging in Christian ethical decision making. Chapters 2 through 4 provide illustrations of each of these aspects of the story-linking process. The starting point in each of these chapters is a key component of our lives that gives shape to our everyday stories that can have either facilitating or inhibiting effects on our liberation and vocation. In chapter 2, we will consider our identity and the social contexts that shape our stories. Chapter 3 focuses on the interpersonal relationships and events that fashion our stories. The meanings we assign to our lives and the direction we envision for our lives, or our unfolding story plot, frame the story-linking process in chapter 4.

We have already given some attention to the significance of Scripture in the lives of African American Christians and its role in story-linking. But, how do we select biblical stories/texts to be used in the process and prepare for their use? Chapter 5 proposes answers to this question in order that participants in Christian education can see its impact on our lives and discern ways of embodying its message in our lives.

Because story-linking is envisioned as a face-to-face group process, it is important that we look carefully at what is needed to guide groups through it in caring ways. In chapter 6, we will explore group processes and dynamics that are helpful in implementing the story-linking model.

CHAPTER 1

A STORY-LINKING PROCESS

The roots of trees spread out in many directions—seeking always seeking the ground of existence for themselves . . . . They [are] on the hunt—for life.

—Howard Thurman
Disciplines of the Spirit

O n many occasions, I have invited groups into a story-linking process by sharing a personal story. One of those times came shortly after a chain of events that brought unfathomable responsibilities and challenges to our family. I shared with the group that the sequence of our story began with the ring of the telephone and a message that was simply: "Mom and Pop [my husband's parents] can no longer stay alone in their home. Their health is such that someone in the family must assure a place of care for them, and a decision must be made soon."

I continued: "After much discussion with our parents and siblings as well as exploration of potential caregiving locations, preparations were made for Mom and Pop to come to live with their son and me. Our parents were in their eighties and understandably wary of relinquishing their own place of independent living. Our concerns centered on whether we would be able to help ease their movement from a known past to an unanticipated present and a future of failing health. We worried about finding appropriate in-home supports needed during our work hours. Our question to ourselves also became: 'Will we be able to meet the challenge of moving from the point where we were in our lives to the realities of the present and into an unknown future?' After our parents had been with us for a while, the poignancy of the question deepened when my husband was rushed into open-heart surgery, and my brother underwent heart bypass surgery the same day. This situation was followed a few months later by another brother's kidney transplant surgery and the diagnosis of cancer received by my husband's brother."

What I wanted the group to know was that at points such as these, really, the questions surface powerfully: "Why is this happening? How do we move through the raging 'storms' on this journey called life? What makes possible our movement from one point to another in the midst of the storm?" Then, I simply asked the group members to choose a partner and share a time in their lives when they asked similar questions.

Even though the group engaged in a lengthy time of sharing, there was the need to continue on. My invitation was to do so by reflecting on the Scripture passage found in the Gospel of Mark, 4:35-41:

> On that day, when evening had come, he said to them, "Let us go across to the other side." And leaving the crowd behind, they took him with them in the boat, just as he was. Other boats were with him. A great windstorm arose, and the waves beat into the boat, so that the boat was already being swamped. But he was in the stern, asleep on the cushion; and they woke him up and said to him, "Teacher, do you not care that we are perishing?" He woke up and rebuked the wind, and said to the sea, "Peace! Be still!" Then the wind ceased, and there was a dead calm. He said to them, "Why are you afraid? Have you still no faith?" And they were filled with great awe and said to one another, "Who then is this, that even the wind and the sea obey him?"

I invited the entire group, first, to hear the biblical story and as they listened, to place themselves in the unfolding scenes. I then asked the partners to read the story to each other while the listening partner placed his- or herself inside the story. This second reading was followed by a dramatization of the story by group members. The third reading was silent and undertaken individually, for the purpose of discerning meanings of the story for our own experiences of the "storms" of life and insights for answering the questions raised in those "storms." An exchange of insights by partners followed this final reading.

A period for whole-group "talk back" resulted in persons' sharing that there are, in fact, times when as Christians, we experience a "sleeping Jesus," but that we need not liken this state with an absent Jesus. My response and that of several other group members was about the times when we felt an inexplicable "presence" that made possible our movement, though slowly, from one point in our lives to another. Others added that Jesus sometimes "stilled their storms" in miraculous ways, but most often came "with skin on" through friends, neighbors, or pastors who were present on the scene, prayed, helped, and in their actions "stilled the storm." Still others spoke of their experience of simply waiting on the Lord and being of good courage, as the song says,[1] and of knowing deep down inside that Jesus is present and "God didn't bring us this far to leave us," as another song makes clear.[2] There were also those who requested prayer for a way through a present "storm."

I continued by sharing with the group that during the difficult circumstances in my family's life, I remembered the story told to me by my parents of one of Harriet Tubman's harrowing trips with several black forebears on the way from slavery to freedom through the Underground Railway. The story that had been handed down to them was that during the trip, the freedom seekers encountered rain, sleet, hail, wind, and cold. Their clothes were tattered and soaked. The soles of their feet gradually took the place of the disappearing soles of their shoes. They ran out of rations. Hunger overtook them. Several in the party sat down on the ground and said to Harriet that they simply could not go on through the storm.

Harriet, who became known as the Moses of our people, looked down at them and said quietly but firmly, "Get up and move," knowing that if they did not do so, they would be found and likely beaten or killed, and the way ahead would be discovered. When they remained seated and cried out their inability to go on, Harriet replied with a bit firmer tone, "Get up and move." Following the continued protestations of those seated on the ground, Harriet reached into her cloak, pulled out a gun, pointed it at the protesters, and said resolutely, "Move or die!" They moved!

In follow-up to both the Bible story and the story about Harriet Tubman, my question to the group was: "What do these stories say to us in our stories of moving from one point to another in our lives in the midst of the storms of adversity?" One of the most powerful statements given by a group member was that "to give up on ourselves and on life is tantamount to pronouncing our own death. We don't see a way out. So, our boat sinks and we drown. Sometimes that happens. Another way to put it is that we don't need Harriet's gun pointed at us. In essence, we point it at ourselves and sometimes 'shoot ourselves in the foot,' meaning we stop ourselves in our tracks and don't get anywhere. But, we must not allow ourselves to do this. We must and we can get up and move! I do it by calling on the name of the Lord daily, knowing that I'm going to get an answer and strength to help others to move. One of the clear messages I got was to become a mentor for young men in my community so they won't get stopped in their tracks. I guess you would say I got called to make a difference."

This response provided an important opening to my closing invitation to the group members to decide on ways of continuing to get up and move.

Envisioning the Process

My approach to story-linking, which I just shared, is not new. My parents used it in our family story times. It was used in the church of my childhood. And, in my travels to Africa, I discovered it continues to be a commonly used process. Yet, although story-linking has cultural roots, it is not always incorporated to any great extent in contemporary African American Christian education contexts. My point in this book is that a vital Christian education for liberating wisdom and hope-building vocation is one that offers a process that has at its center our lived stories. That is, the starting point of Christian education for liberating wisdom and hope-building vocation should be the everyday life stories we face. Such a process should make possible our arriving at insights, discerning choices, and making ethical decisions—wise decisions about what is right to do to promote and sustain liberation for ourselves and others. The process should also enable us to arrive at insights, discern choices, and make the kinds of ethical decisions that lead to our involvement in vocation that centers on and brings a sense of hope in what often seems to be hopeless life situations.

A process that enables these actions is one that links us to the Story of God and the good news of Jesus Christ told in Scripture. A vital Christian education must be forthright in asking the questions: What is it that the Christian story in Scripture has to offer? How may Scripture inform our choices and decisions as African Americans about what is right to do to bring about liberating wisdom that leads to liberation and the enactment of authentic and hope-building Christian vocation? To address these questions is to respond to our deepest needs for God's presence and direction in our liberation and vocational quest. By choosing and entering Bible stories/texts that reveal the hardships and sufferings of an earlier people and God's activity in the midst of anguish, we are enabled to envision God's presence and activity now. We are enabled to envision ourselves, as did those in earlier times, in an unfolding story that is undertaken on faith and in faith and in faithful, hopeful cooperation with God's direction.

The intent of Christian education for liberating wisdom that leads to liberation and hope-building vocation is to place us in touch with our African American forebears' faith and their experience of God's action in their liberating wisdom and hope-building vocation. Linking with our forebears' story helps to inspire us and to foster our commitment to continue on the Christian faith walk. This linkage also promotes our openness and expectation to be continually formed and informed by the Story of God and the good news of Jesus Christ.

Of particular importance are exemplars from the African American heritage who struggled with and overcame tremendous blocks to liberation and who engaged in the kind of ethical decision making that led them into hope-filled vocation. Also, of particular importance are predecessors who interpreted and acted on difficult and oppressive life issues by identifying with stories/texts found in Scripture. Our intent is to see as applicable to ourselves what it meant for them to place their lives in dialogue with Bible stories/texts. We want to see how they made a connection between life hoped for and life valuable enough to continue striving for, and what this means for us today.

In short, in Christian education from an African American perspective, three primary stories are integral parts of the story-linking process: (1) the stories of our everyday lives, (2) the story of God and the good news of Jesus Christ in Scripture, and (3) postbiblical Christian faith heritage stories, particularly those from the African American Christian faith heritage. The task is to engage African Americans in story-linking in ways that help us reflect critically on our particular life stories in light of the Christian faith story. A second task is to guide us as African Americans toward envisioning and deciding actions that hold promise for our forming liberating wisdom that moves us toward liberation and hope-building vocation in the midst of our particular life situations.

The intent in the remainder of this chapter will be to give some direction on how story-linking may be included in Christian education contexts. Attention will be given to a definition of story-linking, the process for story-linking, a process summary, and the importance of compassionate listening.

A Definition of Story-Linking

A definition of story-linking builds on the three primary stories identified above. Specifically, story-linking is a process whereby we connect parts of our everyday stories with the Christian faith story in the Bible and the lives of exemplars of the Christian faith outside the Bible. In this process, we link with Bible stories by using them as mirrors through which we reflect critically on the liberation we have already found or are still seeking, as well as glean wisdom that guides our ongoing liberation efforts. We also link with our Christian faith heritage by learning about exemplars who chose a hope-building way of living based on the liberating wisdom and understanding of vocation they found in Scripture. By linking with Christian faith heritage stories, we may be encouraged and inspired by predecessors who have faced the circumstances with which we readily identify.

The story-linking process can help us open ourselves to God's call to act in ways that are liberating for us and others and to decide how we will do this. It can also help us discern our vocation, formed and informed by the Christian story, as well as ways of accomplishing it.

Engaging the Story-Linking Process

Story-linking is comprised of four primary phases: (1) engaging the everyday story, (2) engaging the Christian faith story in the Bible, (3) engaging Christian faith stories from the African American heritage, and (4) engaging in Christian ethical decision making. Each of the four phases will be discussed in more detail in the following sections.

Phase One: Engaging the Everyday Story

We either consciously or unconsciously use our own personal stories as a lens through which we view what is being focused on in Christian education. We interpret the Bible, struggle with its meaning, and respond to God's word contained in it in light of the realities and demands of our everyday lives. We look at our lives in comparison to the lives of our predecessors and to the ways they lived the Christian story. By placing our stories up front, the intention is not to compromise the importance of the Christian faith story disclosed in the Bible. Rather, the intent is to acknowledge that Christian education leaders/teachers and participants already have an agenda when they come to Christian education. Our stories are the agenda we bring to our study of the Christian faith story in the Bible and our Christian faith heritage.

We may rightly ask: On what should the disclosure of everyday life stories of African Americans focus? The story of my family shared earlier focused on a series of life events. But, life events are by no means all that make up our everyday life stories. There are a number of key components of our lives that give shape to our everyday stories. I am proposing six broad, interrelated factors that contribute to our stories and that can have either facilitating or inhibiting effects on our liberation and vocation. A description of each of the six appears below. As you read each description, consider briefly your own story.

IDENTITY

Our stories are shaped by who we perceive ourselves to be as we continue to relate with the world around us. This includes the personal and cultural identity that becomes ours at birth and about which we form perceptions as we go about our lives in our ethnic cultural context and the larger social context. Our self-identity is how we answer the question: Who am I?

SOCIAL CONTEXTS

Our stories are shaped by the social contexts in which we live and engage in the affairs of life. Where we live, work, and attend school and church; what these places look and feel like; and what larger society feels like are all parts of the social contexts that help to shape our stories. The quality of our social contexts is informed by the availability or nonavailability of needed resources, as well as by kinds and extent of opportunities to participate in them.

Our social contexts are also related to our self-identities. We see ourselves in certain ways in accordance with the qualities comprising our social contexts. We perceive ourselves as like or different from others on the basis of our social contexts. We may also feel ourselves valued or devalued by others on the basis of the social contexts in which we live out our lives.

INTERPERSONAL RELATIONSHIPS

Our stories are shaped by our past and present relationships with persons. These relationships take place in the various social contexts mentioned above. We relate to family members and friends in home and community. We relate to others in church, school, community, and the workplace. We relate to people who are distantly known to us in the political realm and in public media. As Christians, we relate to God through Jesus Christ.

LIFE EVENTS

Our stories are informed by life events taking place in our social contexts and emerging out of our relationships that remain vivid in our memories. Life events are positive and negative incidents that happen to us over the course of our lives. They include incidents we celebrate, crises, and other kinds of incidents that cause concern, hardship, or suffering.

LIFE MEANINGS

Our stories are informed by the meanings we assign to our lives. Our meaning-making is, in fact, our way of making sense out of our lives through judgments we make about every aspect of our lives. Our meaning-making includes both our thoughts and our feelings about our lives. It includes positive and negative thoughts and feelings about our value and dignity as human beings. In meaning-making, we also ponder the source of our positive or negative valuing of ourselves. It also includes what we consider to be the purpose of our lives and what we think and feel about that purpose.

OUR UNFOLDING STORY PLOT

We approach life and act on life according to the meanings we assign to all of the above components of our lives. In addition, how we choose to act contributes to how every part of our lives unfolds. This makes up our unfolding story plot. We may see life optimistically and approach it in positive and constructive ways, or we may see life in negative terms and approach it in destructive ways. How we see life becomes the under-girding theme in our lives and strongly influences how we act. This gives unique character to our unfolding plot.

In the story-linking process in an actual Christian education context, the entry point can be any one of the aforementioned factors that inform the everyday stories of African Americans. Or no more than two factors may be combined. I have found helpful combining identity with life con-texts, interpersonal relationships with life events, and life meanings with unfolding story plots.

In focusing on the paired factors, our intent is to consider critically where liberating wisdom is needed. We are to consider where liberation and hope-filled vocation are facilitated and where they are blocked.

Because the participants in our Christian education contexts may not have had frequent invitation to self-disclosure, they may need to be assured of their right to choose or not choose to share. In the actual process of story-linking, there also may be persons who do not feel com-fortable sharing the details of their stories or who are, in the beginning, reluctant to do so. To ensure the maximum engagement of participants, a case study method is helpful. Through this method, a preconstructed everyday story is presented that focuses on a particular factor in everyday life. The first phase of the story-linking process evolves from the segment of the case that is presented. Upcoming chapters will illustrate how case material may be used. The leader's self-disclosure of a personal story may also append the case study method. For example, this chapter began with an occasion in which I shared a family story. However, when leaders offer personal stories, care must be taken to honor the expressed confidential-ity of family members and to assess the purpose and usefulness of self-disclosure in the story-linking process.

As groups become increasingly comfortable with the process and begin to adopt the process as their own, they may provide their own firsthand experiences as the basis for story-linking. However, uses of case studies or the leader's self-disclosed story at the outset helps free persons to see and talk about themselves through someone else's story. Through case studies or personal illustrations, it is possible for persons to see in their own lives and the lives of group members valuable insights that can be beneficial to their liberation and vocational quests. But, to facilitate this, it is impor-tant that leaders/teachers assure free-flowing and open group sharing.

This means actively discouraging any expression or contribution that comes across as a put-down.

Three activities comprise phase one. They include the everyday story disclosure, the group's critical reflection on the story, and discussion about how group members identify with the story.

Phase Two: Engaging the Christian Faith Story in the Bible

In phase two of the story-linking process, the case study or personally shared material is linked with the Story of God and the good news of Jesus Christ found in Scripture. Recall in my family story presented at the beginning of this chapter that I invited the group to look at the Bible story of Jesus' and the disciples' experience in a storm while crossing over to the other side of a lake. The group engaged the passage from the Gospel of Mark through the lens of their own stories. The Bible story in turn provided the basis for the group to reflect on their life events and struggles through the lens of faith. Group members used the Bible story as a mirror and entered into partnership with the story. They saw in the story how God acts in life, and they envisioned and anticipated how they would cooperate with God.

Using Scripture passages that are already provided in printed lesson materials is a helpful way of engaging Scripture in the story-linking process. However, if this approach is used, it is important to give specific thought to how the passage applies to a specific area of the everyday life story of African Americans. The leader/teacher will need to review the passage and the lesson material to glean from it the particular factor in African American life it addresses and what specific guidance it might provide. This is looking at Scripture through contextual lenses. This is done in preparation for a group session and in tandem with the selection or creation of a case study or other illustrative material. This is important in order that participants may see in the Scripture God's actions in the liberation and vocation of early Christians and what this action has to say for them.

The leader/teacher may also develop the story-linking process focused on a Bible story or text that responds to particular issues raised in the life facet she or he chooses for consideration. As in the preceding situation, the leader/teacher probes the scripture using contextual lenses. She or he chooses case studies or other examples that illustrate everyday struggles.

The scripture is chosen specifically because it addresses concretely the nature of God's action and provides wisdom the African American Christian seeks in her or his quest for liberation and hope-filled vocation.

Another approach to selecting scripture is to draw on the biblical frames of reference used by Christian education participants. Participants in Christian education who have a long history of Bible study and reliance on the Bible for life direction may operate quite naturally out of a biblical frame of reference. Often beginning in childhood, these persons have gained knowledge and understanding of the Bible and have looked to the Bible to address the realities of their lives. Bible stories are primary means through which they find meaning in their lives. They are able to cite specific Bible stories or the roles of certain Bible characters that have directed their experiences and behavior.[3]

In order to use this approach, the leader/teacher needs to be aware that there are participants in the group who come from a Bible-rich tradition and have developed a biblical frame of reference. If this is known, the leader/teacher may invite persons to share Bible passages that have given them direction in specific situations. The leader/teacher may also select Bible stories that address directly the life situation under discussion. In both instances, however, it is important to have on hand a set of Bible commentaries to assist in the exploration of the biblical material. Some examples of how Bible passages may be used in the story-linking process will appear in upcoming chapters.

Five activities are suggested as means of guiding participants in phase two of the story-linking process. In these activities, the Bible story is disclosed; participants focus on the story or text as mirror; they enter into partnership with the characters of the Bible story; they envision God's action today; and they anticipate their ongoing response to God.

Phase Three: Engaging Christian Faith Stories from the African American Heritage

Phase three of the story-linking process is designed to link components of the everyday life story with African American Christian faith heritage stories. In my earlier mentioned family story, the group connected their reflections not only with Scripture but also with the story of Harriet Tubman, a noted figure in the cultural history of African Americans. The group gained understanding and inspiration from the liberation and vocation themes in the midst of trials and tribulation on which the story centered and which lie at the heart of the gospel proclaimed in Scripture. They recognized that the journey of forebears was difficult, but that it was not allowed to thwart efforts to continue on in faith and to lead others in a hope-filled direction. Although we would not likely espouse the current use of the same drastic means appropriated by Harriet Tubman to get persons to move, the story nonetheless conveyed the tenacity of faith and hope needed in tough times.

Of course there are numerous Christian faith heritage stories with which we may connect as part of the story-linking process. Through connecting with these stories, we find an ethical stance on which hope-filled decisions and actions were made and could still be made even when persons experience their backs against the wall. In short, African American Christian faith heritage stories convey a liberating wisdom and liberation mind-set that were at the center of the Christian life of African Americans in the past and that are worthy of emulation in the present.

How do we choose the story? There are numerous collections of literature focused on African American history that tell of our predecessors' religious lives. In choosing what to use in the story-linking process, however, it is important to identify those sources in which the stories are told by African Americans themselves. It is important to be aware that stories may be told in a variety of ways and through a variety of approaches. This means that we should not be hesitant in seeking and using stories, music, sermons, poems, prayers, and artwork that give voice to the African American Christian faith heritage. Some examples will be used in upcoming chapters.

Christian education participants will also have knowledge of heritage stories that they have been taught and that have provided past insight and encouragement to them. These stories will include not only stories of African American heroes and heroines well known to most African Americans but also stories of family heroes and heroines. This personal treasury of heritage stories should not be overlooked. Rather, these stories bring added meaning and depth to the story-linking process.

Three activities are suggested as means of guiding participants in phase three of the story-linking process. The activities are aimed toward assisting participants in identifying how African American predecessors lived out the Christian faith story on which the gospel message of the Bible centers. In these activities, the Christian faith heritage story is disclosed; participants discern and describe the liberating wisdom and liberation mind-set found in the story; and they describe the liberation and vocational strategy found in the story.

Phase Four: Engaging in Christian Ethical Decision Making

Activities in phase four of the story-linking process are designed to guide persons in exploring options for liberating and Christian vocational actions that have constructive, or what is understood as hope-building, outcomes for them and for others. In this phase, persons bring to bear on their life stories ideas, wise insights, and discernment from the first three phases of the story-linking process. In my opening story to this chapter, a group member described the inability of some persons to act in hope-building ways in the lives of self and others. He then told of the necessity of countering this inert behavior with constructive action and of his call to act.

If Christian education activities are to result in liberating wisdom that moves persons toward liberation and hope-building vocation, they must give attention to meanings of and commitment to faithful and responsible Christian action. These activities assume that we as African Americans have a continuing stake in the liberation and vocational direction of others.

We move toward being faithful and responsible as well as toward liberation and vocation as we claim the story of God and the good news of Jesus Christ found in the Bible as our own. But above all, we move in this direction when we allow ourselves to be shaped by that story and are assured that God is acting in our lives. It means discerning and reflecting critically on how we may intentionally cooperate with this activity. And it means deciding on what and how we will be and act in partnership with God and knowing why. When we engage ourselves in these ways, we are wholly involved in Christian ethical decision making.

Participants become involved in two activities in phase four. In these activities, they discern God's call for concrete liberating and vocational action, and they decide concrete actions.

A Summary of the Entire Story-Linking Process

The story-linking process entails four phases that follow in sequence. Activities facilitate each phase and are designed to be followed in sequence. The entire process need not be covered in one session. If you choose to complete all four phases in one session, it should take about one and one-half hours. If you prefer shorter time segments, complete phases one and two in one session and phases three and four in the next session. The total process is shown below. It is further illustrated in chapters 2, 3, and 4.

Phase One: Engage the Everyday Story
    Activity 1. Disclose the Everyday Story
    Activity 2. Critically Reflect on Case or Other Illustrative
         Material
    Activity 3. Identify with the Case Study or Other Illustrative
         Material

Phase Two: Engage the Christian Faith Story in the Bible
    Activity 1. Disclose the Bible Story/Text
    Activity 2. Focus on the Bible Story as Mirror
    Activity 3. Enter as Partner with Bible Story Actors
    Activity 4. Envision God's Activity Today
    Activity 5. Anticipate Ongoing Response to God

Phase Three: Engage Christian Faith Stories from the African
         American Heritage
    Activity 1. Disclose the Faith Heritage Story
    Activity 2. Describe the Liberating Wisdom and Liberation Mind-
         Set
    Activity 3. Describe Liberation and Vocational Strategies

Phase Four: Engage in Christian Ethical Decision Making
    Activity 1. Discern God's Call for Concrete Action
    Activity 2. Decide Concrete Actions

The Importance of Compassionate Listening

We dare not envision Christian education processes without giving serious thought to the quality of settings in which the processes are to occur. It is not enough to say simply that we will carry out the processes. The emotional environment will have much to do with the success or failure of what we attempt to do.

It is my position that we need to do more to make African American Christian education settings nurturing spaces. We need to ensure spaces wherein persons are given voice and can enter into dialogue together in open, caring, and supportive ways. It is important to create spaces where intergenerational dialogue can take place and where socioeconomic differences are transcended. This is an important approach to fulfilling a vision of community where all are considered mutual sojourners.

If we are to be truly emancipatory and focused on hope-filled vocation, we must be intentional in our embodiment of the Christian story in the Christian education settings we fashion. This embodiment can happen only as we begin to envision what it means to express *agape love*. This is love that dares to hear others, to enter into the experiences of others, to feel with others their concerns and sufferings, and to envision and anticipate with others ways of confronting their concerns and sufferings. To do this is to engage in *inliving*, or living in solidarity with others.[4] This deeply felt sense of solidarity makes it possible for persons to be sustained in their discernment of liberating wisdom that assists the kind of liberation and hope-building vocation described in the prologue.

Embodying the Christian story through *inliving* must also include compassionate listening. When we listen compassionately, we show a genuine interest in the concerns and the sufferings of others. As a listening presence, we are also called to be sensitive to the difficulty persons often have in disclosing and confronting life struggles. Compassionate listening is part of creating an environment in which persons feel comfortable to share. When persons feel comfortable enough to share and are encouraged to speak, their stories expose the self. In compassionate listening, the sharing of self is regarded as gift and is received with great caring and sensitivity.

In short, an important task to be undertaken in the story-linking process is to ensure an environment that contains the emancipatory qualities that can foster persons' liberation and enactment of hope-building vocation outside that setting.

Reflection Exercise

Consider the group(s) you will engage in the story-linking process. Envision what is needed to create a nurturing space for story-sharing and compassionate listening. How will you make agape love and inliving central to the story-linking process?

CHAPTER 2

EXPLORING SELF AND WORLD THROUGH STORY-LINKING

*Often it is most difficult to accept our fact. Such acceptance means to say
"yes" to that which is our own bill of particulars. . . . It means being very specific about ourselves. This is our face, not another's; it will always be our face
exhibiting a countenance that reveals all the laughter and all the tears of our
years of living. . . . No substitute can be found for it—go wherever we will,
knock at every door, our face remains our face.*

—Howard Thurman
The Inward Journey

T he African American story is about a people who continue to ask,
"Who am I?" in the midst of society's assaults on our dignity. The
question Who am I? centers on our self-identity, and that identity
is shaped in the many spheres we carry out in our everyday lives.

When we arrive at positive notions of self-identity, we regard ourselves
as valued human beings. As Christians this means we see ourselves
through the eyes of God found in Jesus Christ revealed in Scripture. We
see our lives as gifts from God, and we see what we have to give to others. Our positive view of who we are liberates us to be positive forces in
the lives of others. It frees us to be in hope-building vocation for our own
and others' lives. We go about our lives as Christians with intentionality
and expectancy of our role as contributors to the well-being of others.

Our negative self-identity blocks this ability to be positive forces in others' lives. It blocks our vocation.

Where and how do we develop our identities? The answer lies in a critical consciousness of the world we live in including our families, communities, and larger social contexts. These social contexts of our lives inform how we regard ourselves. We must be attentive to the positive views liberated in us as we interact with others in these contexts. Most especially, we must see the valued selves that we are in spite of assaults to our value and dignity; and we must nullify the self-views that counter the value God places on us and thereby block our liberation and vocation. Our challenge is to build on the positives and see our need to be freed from the negatives. Our challenge is to seek and embrace a liberating wisdom that results in an ongoing inner surety of our human value and our knowing deeply God's value of *all* persons revealed in Scripture.

In this chapter, we enter the story-linking process by examining the formation of our identities in the world we live in, including our families, communities, and larger society. We will look at our identities in light of case studies of members of two families. One story is told by a family member whom we will call Mary Johnson. The other is told by a family member whom we will call Ken Brown. Our purpose is to recall our own stories in order to become conscious of the views of ourselves we have formed and whether these identities foster or inhibit our own and others' liberation and vocation.

We will link our self-identity stories with a Bible passage with which African Americans resonate because of its focus on identity struggles in difficult and oppressive social contexts and its disclosure of wisdom to address the struggles. We will also link with a faith heritage story that encapsulates the nature of the African American identity struggle and presents a faith response and wise approach to the struggle.

An important assumption underlies this chapter. The assumption is that liberating wisdom is needed for our seeing and embracing the value of ourselves given by God. Moreover, the assumption is that when we value ourselves the way God values us, we open ourselves to a variety of dimensions of liberation. We begin to see possibilities we had not heretofore imagined. We become better able to perceive not only who and Whose we are, but also who we can become. We also open ourselves to hope-building vocation, which is our response to God's call to care for others in ways that build up and sustain their valued self-views.

We learned earlier that the story-linking process has four phases, each of which incorporates several activities. The disclosure of two case studies begins the process in phase one.

Phase One: Engage the Everyday Story

The case study material presented below and case material in subsequent chapters will help us focus on self-identity, social context, interpersonal relationships, life events, and life meanings. However, specific attention is given here to the nature and formation of self-identity in social contexts. The names in the case studies are fictitious.

Case Study 1: Mary Johnson's Story Then and Now

When I talked with Mary Johnson in her home sometime ago, she was watching her daughter at the desk across the room. The desk was filled with opened books, and her daughter was busily writing a paper for school. Mary's face shone with pride as she told about her daughter's hard work and academic accomplishments. She shared:

> "You know, it's not easy for our young people today. Well, I guess it never has been. But, my husband and I have done our best to provide for our children. We've prayed a lot. It's not easy being parents either. But, when you're a parent—well, you have to *be* a parent. There are things in my life that I wish I could have changed, but being the mother of my children isn't one of them. All in all, I've found being a parent is rewarding. I'd have to say that I'm probably my most caring self as a mother.
>
> "I remember when I was growing up. My parents always said, 'Never forget to stand up straight and hold your head up. Be proud of who you are.' It wasn't just a thing of posture. They were letting me know that I was a worthwhile person and that I had a heritage to be proud of. Their words have remained with me, and I've tried to instill the same in my children. One thing I also learned from my parents and in church is that other people can try to stop us, but we can't let them. We can't escape the fact that we're African Americans. That's who we are. And, even though living life in these skins of ours is not easy, we know God made us this way and we're valuable in God's sight. I'm a teacher, too, and I try to get this across to my students.

"Oh, I've run into obstacles along the way. And I can't deny that, at times, they made a real mark on my self-image. I remember when students were being considered for the National Honor Society in the predominantly white high school I attended. I was always on the honor roll and participated in a lot of school activities. My goal was to be tops, and I was a high achiever. But I was not chosen for the Honor Society. I found out that some of my white classmates whose grade averages were lower than mine were chosen. It was a terrible blow to me. I can remember crying and crying on my bed at home. I hated who I was, and I frankly thought, 'Why bother ever trying to excel and to be somebody again.' All my parents' talk about standing up straight and being proud went out the window, at least at that specific point in time.

"But, the main thing was that I really didn't let the situation in that high school stop me cold. In fact, I credit that situation with pushing me toward becoming a teacher. I wanted to be in a position to help others and, when I could, to counter negative influences on their lives.

"There were other things, too. How I thought about myself for a long time had a lot to do with an experience at home early in my life. When I was four or five years old, my brother suddenly stopped relating to me. He would not talk to me, sit beside me, or come near me in any way. His treatment of me didn't change until I was grown. I didn't understand why this was happening and whenever I would ask, my parents would simply tell me not to let it bother me. I felt as though there was something terribly wrong with me. And I felt abandoned by my brother, whom I idolized.

"It was not until I was grown that I found out that my brother had been taken aside and severely scolded for playing too roughly with me. His response to the scolding was to completely ignore me for fear of getting into trouble again. But I do think that because of what happened, I'm much more demonstrative in showing affection than I might have been otherwise. And, I think it made me sensitive to others' needs to be included and loved. I also think the whole thing had a big effect on my brother's estimation of himself. Even today, it is hard for him to show affection to anyone. He really became a bottled-up person.

"There are things I have done, too, both good and not so good, that have affected how I think about myself. I mean, some of the things I have chosen to do, like my volunteer work at a senior center some years ago, gave me a kind of peace within myself and positive acceptance of myself as having something to give. At other times, I have not felt okay within myself because I wasn't doing all I could do to help myself and other people, or because I had done something wrong and hadn't set things straight.

"I wrestle with myself even more—with who I am, what I ought to be, and how to get unstuck—when I get into one of those places that triggers self-doubt. Deep down inside, though, I see myself as a good person. And, even when I have doubts, I know that God knows who I am. Regardless of what others think or do and, really, regardless of my own getting in my own way, I believe God sees me as valuable. I just need to be reminded about that every now and then. And, I need to be reminded that God is there for me when I come upon those obstacles about self-doubt.

"Today, as I think about these earlier memories of mine, I'd simply have to say how revealing they are of my past and present. But, now, after so many years as a teacher, I am so much more aware of the challenge to positive identities our young people face. I see the self-denigration of children who experience maltreatment or neglect at home. It seems to me that families act out of negative understandings of what they ought to be like. Of course, I also see those who think poorly of themselves as the result, I think, of their experiences of their neighborhood, society—and even the school—as hostile, hurting places. I ask the questions more than ever before: 'What is to become of us as a people? How is it possible for us to know and act on our goodness even while we live in environments that fail to honor that goodness?' Well, I really think it's my responsibility as a Christian and as a teacher not simply to search for answers to the questions, but to make the answers come alive in what I do with others."

Case Study 2: Ken Brown's Story Then and Now

My earlier conversation with Ken Brown took place in my office where he leaned forward, then back, and heaved many quiet long sighs as he began to tell his story:

"There's no doubt about it, getting this far in my life has been hard; and I'm still young. In my family, I was the youngest of seven children.

My dad died when I was about three years old. So, basically, my mom had her hands full. We lived on the poor side of town. I mean it was *real poor*. Mom worked in a dry cleaners, and my oldest sister worked part-time after she got out of high school each day. She also worked on weekends. Even so, it just wasn't enough. There's not much to say about who we were, except that we were poor and we felt like we were society's castaways. We were trying to make it against the odds.

"We wore hand-me-down clothes that were beyond mending, and we didn't always have shoes that kept our feet off the ground, if you know what I mean. We had food stamps, but, still, food stretching was an ordinary thing; and my mother always talked about how nasty the store clerks were when she would hand them the stamps.

"I can remember Mom was a proud person, and she tried to do her best with us kids. She tried to make us behave. She tried to make us stay in school. She tried to make us study. Sometimes, she'd get very upset with us kids—you know how kids can be and what it must have been like to have seven of us. But she'd always say, 'Everything's gonna be all right. We're gonna make it with God's help.' If there ever was a person who had hope, she was it. I can't say that I believed as she did when I was growing up. It just seemed to me then that we got the raw end of the deal in life. We didn't go to church or Sunday school or anything like that, but we always said grace at the dinner table. I also remember many times hearing Mom praying while she was fixing a meal, trying to clean up the house, and doing other things around the house. Now that I think of it, I guess she had to pray in order for her to keep going in a house with seven kids.

"I really believe my mom's pride, her hope, her desire for the best for all of us, and her prayers made a difference in my life. It didn't seem to make a difference for some of my brothers and sisters, but it did for me. Now, I did get into my share of mischief, especially in elementary school, and I was suspended several times. But I know something must have made a difference because I made it through school. Or maybe I should say I chose to survive in a different way. I'm the only one in my family who became a churchgoer. Don't get me wrong. I don't fault them. It's just that there's something I've got to do. I've committed my life as a Christian to ministry with young people in situations like mine.

"I know some folk don't think anything good can come out of the poor section of town, and that poor folk don't help themselves or anybody else. That may be true for some. But that's not true for all.

There are proud, hardworking, poor folk who want things to be different and who are working to make things different for themselves and others. My mom was one of those folk. And so am I. I am worried about several of my brothers and sisters, though, because they can't seem to get beyond all the negatives. It is sometimes hard not to get discouraged when I think of them. I do what I can, but sometimes I think, 'How can I feel good about being who I am now when they are having such trouble?' "

Ken moved away sometime after the meeting in which he shared his story. His intent was to establish a ministry with troubled youth. One day my phone rang and, upon answering it, I heard the voice of someone who identified themselves as a friend of Ken's. The friend told of being asked by Ken to call me to ask prayer for Ken. Things had not seemed to turn out as Ken had hoped. In fact, the shadow of his past seemed to loom over him like a dark cloud. He had come to a point of questioning his worth, his abilities, and his call. Ken's friend said, "I don't know what the outcome of all of this will be. Just pray for him. And, pray for me that I will know what I can do to help him."

Activity 1—Disclose the Everyday Story

Use of prerecorded tapes of the case studies using African American voices is a helpful method of presentation. Participants may also read the cases aloud—a woman for Mary's story and a man for Ken's story. Or, leader(s)/teacher(s) may read them.

Prior to presenting the cases, invite participants to listen for evidence of positive and negative self-perceptions of Mary and Ken. Encourage participants to:

- Listen for the social contexts—the home and wider community including the church, workplace, school—in which Mary's and Ken's self-perceptions arose;
- Locate circumstances under which the self-perceptions arose;
- Give particular attention to where and in what ways Mary's and Ken's self-identities blocked their enactment of hope-filled vocation and where and what changes in their self-identities liberated this enactment;
- Notice what ongoing challenges to their own and/or others' identity-formation appear in the stories.

Participants should be free to identify issues regarding self-identity the cases raise for them.

Activity 2—Critically Reflect on the Case Material

In activity 2 of phase one of the story-linking process, participants respond to the listening cues indicated above. The approach used for sharing depends on the size of the group and their readiness for open group sharing. In large groups, it is helpful to talk in small groups followed by small group report-backs. In situations where there is a fair amount of reticence in open group sharing, persons may share with a partner. Each small group or pair may choose a reporter to convey insights to the larger group.

Reflection Exercise

Consider your responses to the case studies based on the listening cues given above. Some actual participant responses are as follows:

Self-Identity in Social Context and Liberation and
Vocation of Mary Johnson

> "Mary's present self-identity is tied to her role as mother in the context of home and to the role of teacher in the context of the school. There is a sense in which she is bound to these roles and either cannot envision or did not choose to mention an identity in other contexts."

> "The foundation for Mary's self-identity was laid in the home where she grew up. That foundation had to do with her posture— holding the head high and standing up straight. But it also had to do with maintaining pride in her heritage, who she is as an African American, and seeing herself as valued because God made her the way she is. However, this foundation was challenged in the home and school contexts. Finding a block to her self-identity in school was not surprising. Finding a block in the home was an important reminder that our identities are not formed in just one place."

> "For a long time, Mary needed liberation from her negative views acquired in the home and school. Her story shows that she somehow

got a vision of herself as a caring person and as teacher. She actualized this vision in her home and school. In this way, her vision may be described as a liberating vision, and her enactment of it may be described as her liberation to vocation. We can guess that her early foundation may have made a difference. But we cannot tell whether she came out of a strong positive self-perception or from one that isn't as strong as it might be. This raises the issue of how strong a person's self-identity has to be in order for them to move toward and fulfill vocation. But even when persons have a less than strong self-identity, it does not have to be crippling. Isn't it possible that a person can accomplish a lot in spite of a weak self-identity or even because of it?"

"The issues Mary raises about abusive, neglectful, and outright racist experiences of our young today are real. And there is no question that the impact of these experiences on self-identity and self-worth can be devastating, even to the point of youths' contemplation of or actual suicide. We have to be concerned about this situation. We also have to have a positive and strong enough self-identity to be able to bring some hope in these difficult situations. Mary's on the right track in this regard."

Self-Identity in Social Context and Liberation and Vocation of Ken Brown

"Ken identified himself as a Christian survivor. In this way, he came to a positive view of himself in spite of the views he felt others held of him and his family. Ken definitely internalized the negative views toward the poor found in the larger social context. He may have even taken on these views and 'worn them like a badge.' This perhaps figured into his acting out and being suspended from school. But, like Mary, he was about to build on a foundation he received in the home that included the views that persons are important to God."

"Ken experienced liberation to vocation in spite of his bombardment with negative views from the larger social context. He envisioned a call to take on the identity of minister in order to confront the concerns for a positive self-identity faced by other African Americans. The foundation that was built in the home where Ken grew up contributed to his liberation. But, unlike Mary, he mentioned that one dimension of liberation for him came through religious transformation. This seems to have been highly instrumental in his overcoming the blocks of negative self-identity, because with it he received a new identity.

"There is a question, though, about whether Ken will be overwhelmed with his new identity and whether he will feel guilty for having it to the degree that it becomes a restrictive negative self-perception. His story raises the issue of whether our liberation from an old negative identity to a new positive identity can be threatening and even scary."

"This question raised by others is especially powerful now that we have a glimpse of Ken's unfolding story. What has actually happened to him is not clear, but it certainly seems that something has profoundly threatened his capacity to hold on to the sense of self he developed earlier. This raises the question "What do we do when we experience reversals in our self-identity from the okay self to the not-so-okay self?"

Activity 3—Identify with the Case Study

In activity 3, I invite participants to disclose what the cases evoked in them about their own self-perceptions. Starter questions for this disclosure include:

- In what ways are Mary's and Ken's stories your story?
- What memories of self-perceptions and social contexts did their stories trigger in you?
- How would you respond to the personal and family issues that were raised in the stories? What would you say is the role of the church's identity and activity?
- What comments would you add to the responses of participants reported above, and what answers would you give to the questions those participants raised?

Follow-up questions might include: Did anyone have difficulty relating to the stories? What was difficult? Why was it difficult?

I have found that people tend to key in on one specific aspect of one of the case studies. Some identify with the positive self-perceptions found in Mary's or Ken's case study and then build on that perception to describe how they consider themselves and who contributed to that consideration. Others identify with a particular place, such as Mary's high school, as a way of talking about the social context in which they themselves confronted blocks and formed negative self-perceptions. Participants also tend to use Mary's becoming a teacher and Ken's moving toward ministry with youth as ways of talking about what they themselves are or are not doing with regard to vocation. Some persons also disclose difficulties they themselves have or that others have in arriving at a positive self-identity in social contexts. Indeed, some echo the questions raised in the participants' responses shown earlier and emphasize their need for answers to the questions.

Reflection Exercise

What did the cases evoke in you?

Phase Two: Engage the Christian Faith Story in the Bible

The intent in phase two of the story-linking process is to link Mary's, Ken's, and our own reflections of the cases with Scripture. We seek guidance from Scripture on the formation of self-identity in social context from a Christian standpoint. Our search is accomplished through five activities including aligning with a specific scripture, focusing on the scripture as mirror, entering into partnership with Bible story actors, envisioning God's action today, and anticipating ongoing response to God. Psalm 139 is used here to illustrate a manner of linking with Scripture.

Psalm 139 is a particularly helpful Bible passage for African Americans' exploration of self-identity. In the face of ongoing bombardment of African Americans with negative views from the larger social context and assaults to self-identity elsewhere, the psalm proposes a counterview. It grants African Americans an identity that is not tied to what humans ascribe to it. It anchors identity in God.

Activity 1—Disclose the Bible Story/Text

I invite persons to enter Psalm 139 by considering the questions: Why Psalm 139? What does Psalm 139 have to contribute to our understanding of our self-identities as African Americans in the social contexts described in the case studies and in our lives? These questions provide specific listening cues.

The self-identities of Mary and Ken were formed in contexts where there were both positive experiences and anguished experiences of hurt, alienation, and suffering. Along the way, they both arrived at positive notions of self, but there were also instances in which those notions were challenged. However, both Mary and Ken saw God as Guarantor of their positive self-identities. But they needed to know that this Guarantor can be counted on in the face of doubt and experiences that challenge positive self-identity. The experiences of Mary and Ken are not unlike our own.

I also add that the formation of self-identity in the social contexts in the case studies and the formation of our own self-identities in our social contexts are not unique to us. The important question Who am I? as well as where and how that question gets answered have been posed throughout the history of humankind. It was posed during biblical times. The psalmist who wrote Psalm 139 was among the ancient Israelites who had experienced the troubling and disorienting wilderness sojourn of a people in the years following their exodus from Egypt. The trials and tribulations pushed the psalmist to consider the question of identity. Psalm 139 reveals the psalmist's conversation with God about the answer to the question Who am I in the context in which I find myself? It further discloses the psalmist's discovery of the good news that God knows the psalmist. The identity of the psalmist is tied to this knowing God from whose creative activity the life of the psalmist comes. Psalm 139 affirms the presence of the knowing God and affirms that the psalmist's valued selfhood derives from God, belongs inseparably to God, and that the self finds its true destination in God's purposes.[1]

Participants then hear Psalm 139. There are many creative ways to present Scripture. Like the case studies, Scripture may be presented on a prerecorded audiotape using a single African American voice or several African American voices. It may be read responsively from the Bible, with the leader/teacher and the participants reading alternate verses, or it may be read collectively from large printed placards or newsprint centrally located in a meeting room. Take some time now to read Psalm 139.

Activity 2—Focus on the Bible as Mirror

Invite persons into a second reading of the psalm. During this reading, persons approach the psalm as a mirror in their further exploration of answers to the questions: Who are Mary, Ken, and I in our social contexts? Who are our family, church, and our community? We also consider what constitutes the liberating wisdom in the psalm that can assist us in our liberation struggle and our exercise of hope-filled vocation. Guide this kind of exploration by inviting persons to find the psalm motifs or words that suggest answers to the questions and responses to our search for liberating wisdom. Invite them to describe how these motifs challenge our understanding of liberation and vocation and to voice their own questions that the psalm raises. Provide Bible commentaries or other materials to assist the participants' exploration of the psalm as holding meaning for them.

Reflection Exercise

Enter into a time now to reread Psalm 139 to discover your responses. Responses summarized from actual participants and commentaries are as follows:

> "The psalm is saying that Mary, Ken, and we each have an identity that does not come from what other people say or do in our social contexts. That identity is found in God. The God that the psalmist speaks about is *One who has depthful knowledge* about who we are and what happens to us." (verses 1-12)

> "Regardless of our social contexts, God is always with us, before us, over us, and surrounding us. God leads and holds God's people of faith even in the most difficult trials and tribulations of life. We are transparent to God and known by God, because *God created us*." (verses 13-16)

> "Because we recognize that God created us and knows us, there is nowhere we can go and nothing that can happen to us that can separate our being from God's being. *In God is our identity and our life*." (verses 17-18)

> "God provides a protective reality or a 'sacred canopy,' under which we can feel completely known, secure, affirmed, and loved even in the midst of social contexts that are threatening. Under this 'sacred canopy,' *God hears our prayers and innermost cries*." (verses 19-24)[2]

"God knows us better than we know ourselves. God knows us in a different way than those around us know us. And God knows us longer and deeper than any other. Our identities *are* more, *can be* more, than those which are already known about us.[3] When we see our identity through God's eyes, we are freed to *be* more and to act out of that being. We no longer see our social contexts as binding us."

"The psalm challenges us to look more closely at our *self-perceptions* and our social contexts. We are challenged to address what is preventing us from grounding our identities in God. Of what help is it if we ground our identities in God's and feel liberated by that grounding, but do not seek to change anything in the world? This is a question of vocation."

"The knowing God revealed in the psalm is our way back to positive self-identity and life purpose when we have lost our sense of them. Our knowing that we belong to God provides us the anchoring and strength we need to carry on. We may be able to accomplish a lot in spite of a weak self-identity or even because of it. But that takes a lot of energy—more energy than is needed if we know that *we know* God knows us and gives us not just a valued self-identity but ego-strength to carry on. That's what I would want for myself. I would want the same for my whole family."

Activity 3—Enter as Partner with Bible Story Actors

We begin the third activity by imaging ourselves standing or sitting with the psalmist. From this stance, we enter into conversation with God along with the psalmist, as though the words of Psalm 139 are our own. We then recite the psalm from this partnership stance.

A particularly helpful way of entering this partnership with the psalmist is for two persons to read the psalm together. In pairs, one would assume the role of the psalmist, while the other reads from her/his own personal stance. After the reading, the partners would exchange roles.

Reflection Exercise

Imagine yourself as a partner with the psalmist. Read the words of the psalm as though they were your words being said in partnership with the psalmist.

Activity 4—Envision God's Activity Today

Invite persons to envision God's action in forming and informing our self-identities in our social contexts. Consider also our families' identities. This envisioning process may be accomplished through one or more of the following: (1) Persons may enter into a time of silent reflection in which they envision God's affirming their identity in God. (2) Persons may be invited to share their responses to the impact of reading Psalm 139 as though it were their own words and in partnership with the psalmist. (3) Persons may be asked to write and share a prayer, a poem, a rap or choose a song to sing, draw a picture, or construct a group collage from magazine pictures or original pictures.

These activities should convey something of the meanings persons assign to identities that are grounded in God and their feelings about those meanings. For example, in one instance, the psalm confirmed for a person the meaning of a favorite African American gospel song entitled "God Is." The person then shared the words: "God is the joy and the strength of my life."

Reflection Exercise

Choose and complete one of the three exercises above.

Activity 5—Anticipate Ongoing Response to God

In this final activity of phase two, I invite persons to anticipate their response to God's call to individuals and families and the extended family of the church to anchor their self-identities in God. This entails identifying negative self-perceptions God is calling us to release, both individually and as families. Some starter questions that are helpful to ask are: What negative perceptions do you have of yourself that hinder your acting in liberating ways or in vocation that give and sustain hope in your various social contexts? How did God challenge you through the psalm to release negative self-perceptions? How is your family challenged by the psalm? How is your church challenged by the psalm?

Forming the participants in pairs or in small groups can facilitate sharing in this activity of the story-linking process. Or persons may engage in this activity meditatively. Some persons find it helpful to record what they discern in a journal. If there are persons who wish to share what they discern, however, they should not be prevented from doing so.

Reflection Exercise

Enter into a time of meditation on what God is saying to you about your self-identity. Some actual participant responses are as follows:

"I've always had to work on my perception of myself as not having the ability to measure up. This stems, in part, from an experience in school. When I failed to read a sentence correctly, I was told to sit down and that I 'didn't know beans from potatoes.' For a long time, it blocked my ability to read. I have also had trouble believing in myself, and I tend not to put a great deal of effort into things for fear of failure."

"I am challenged to stop crying over the negative way others define me. I've cried long enough. Sometimes it's hard, but I do have the power to look beyond the words that tear me down. I don't have to let others' opinions become my reality. I also have the responsibility to counter negative comments I hear being made about us whenever I hear them. I also know that I'm not perfect and God knows that too. I have both the power and the responsibility to shape up what isn't right."

"There are some problems in my family that need fixing. It's like I can't do anything right. How can I like myself when nobody else seems to like me? I see and hear what the Scripture is saying to me. It gives me something to hold on to. My family needs to know that what it says is for them, too, so that maybe it could make a difference for all of us."

"It is important that my church be an affirming place. It's a small struggling church, and we get down on ourselves a lot. Unless we see ourselves in the right light, we can't carry out any adequate kind of vocation. I believe that and think church members are called to a better way of seeing ourselves so we can do ministry in a better way."

Phase Three: Engage Christian Faith Stories from the African American Heritage

In phase three of the story-linking process, we link with an African American Christian faith heritage story. Many stories are possible for this stage. What I call "Grandmother's Message About Identity," as told by Howard Thurman, will be used here to illustrate how this linkage can occur in an actual Christian education setting. The story is particularly conducive to the African American focus on self-identity in a *story-linking* process because it shows vividly the similarity between the *self-identity* struggle of our forebears and our own struggle. But more than this, it conveys forcefully our value in God's eyes by daring to utter the opposite view we hear regularly. Grandmother's Message About Identity may be told in this way:

> When I was a youngster, this [sense of identity through God's love] was drilled into me by my grandmother. The idea was given to her by a certain slave minister who, on occasion, held secret religious meetings with his fellow slaves. How everything in me quivered with the pulsing tremor of raw energy when, in her recital, she would come to the triumphant climax of the minister: "You—you are not niggers. You—you are not slaves. You are God's children."[4]

This brief story becomes the basis for the following two activities of phase three: linking with the African American heritage story and describing the liberating wisdom in it, the liberation mind-set, and a hope-filled vocational strategy.

Activity 1—Disclose the Faith Heritage Story

I simply invite persons to enter the context in which Howard Thurman recalls his Grandmother's Message About Identity. We imagine ourselves to be in the grandparent's home. I assign half of the participants to take Howard Thurman's role as narrator and to read the words that introduced what his grandmother said. The other half are asked to read incisively and dramatically Grandmother's precise repetition of the minister's words. Very often, I will ask the two groups to reverse roles, so that each group has a chance to be both the narrator and the grandmother.

As means of connecting the heritage story with our current-day ethos, I invite youth especially to recall the lyrics of rap music that assign to African Americans derogatory labels. This includes the term "nigger" (or "nigga")—the very term that Howard Thurman's grandmother sought to erase as a negative ascription of black identity. My intent is to bring into our exploration of liberating wisdom, liberation, and vocation the question of linguistic practice and whether the artistic style of hip-hop stretches the bounds of African American identity—individually, as male and female, and collectively. My invitation is for participants to struggle with what Michael Eric Dyson calls "flexible readings of text's meanings" and what the *naming* means for the identities of those who hear it, recite it, and may internalize and act on it.[5]

Activity 2—Describe the Liberating Wisdom, Liberation Mind-Set, and Vocational Strategy

Here we explore the liberating wisdom, liberation mind-set, and vocational strategy in Grandmother's Message About Identity. This is done first by considering how Psalm 139 is reflected in the story, given the social context in which it is cast. Persons often respond to this invitation by saying that the story lets us know as African Americans that in spite of the social context in which we feel enslaved, devalued, or denigrated, we are God's creations.

To invite further reflection, additional questions are posed: Would you say that Grandmother's Message contains wisdom that is useful today? Why? How might Grandmother's Message About Identity create a liberation mind-set in persons today? How might the message help us to see ourselves positively and act on that positive view? Is there more that is needed than the story provides to help create in us a liberating mind-set? If so, what is needed? What does it suggest for a hope-filled vocation that includes how we name others? How would you answer these same questions with regard to examples of hip-hop that name African Americans in terms once regarded—and still regarded by some—as derogatory?

Reflection Exercise

Enter into a time now to consider your answers to the above questions. Actual responses of participants to the questions include:

> "The message is a wholly applicable one today since we continue to hear ourselves called by what I consider offensive terms both by persons who are not African American and by African Americans outside and within our homes. The message itself is wise and given by a wise elder."

"The dominant mind-set was one of staunch maintenance of a counterview of self over the one often given to us. The message is a helpful one in that there is a sense in which it is being passed on and on from one generation to another. It reminds me of Jesse Jackson's words: 'I am somebody!' It suggests a strategy of reciting over and over again the countermessage: 'We are God's children!' and, 'I am somebody!' At the same time, there is more to it than simply saying the words. We have to believe it deep down inside. And to come to believe it, we have to keep struggling to combat all the negatives that knock us down and that have an impact on our negative views of ourselves. That is key!"

"I listen to hip-hop a lot and I hear the language in it. Until now, I had not given any thought to the connection between the language and how I think about my identity or anyone else's. I will have to think about it some more. I would have to say, though, that I do not stand for someone who is not African American to call me 'nigger' or any other insulting name. That is strictly out of line. But, again, I'll have to think about that whole thing of in-group name-calling."

Phase Four: Engage in Christian Ethical Decision Making

The aim in the last phase of the story-linking process is decision making regarding actions that can liberate ongoing positive self-identity. To do this, we propose possible and plausible actions that emerge from our discernment of God's call for action.

Activity 1—Discern God's Call

We begin by engaging in what I refer to as "silent memory summation." This entails our calling to memory, silently, as much as we can about Psalm 139 and the story of Grandmother's Message About Identity. After our silent memory summation, I invite group members to choose a partner. The partners share specific points in the psalm and in Grandmother's Message About Identity that motivate them and hold potential for motivating their families and churches to address negative self-identities that surface within and beyond them. Partners also share specific social contexts in which they, their families, and their churches are called to act.

Reflection Exercise

Enter into the silent memory summation. What in Psalm 139 and Grandmother's Message About Identity motivates you to action, and where are you being called to act?

Actual responses of participants are as follows:

"I was motivated by the psalmist's confirmation that wherever I go, God is with me. That is a double-edged motivation for me. I know that if I sit down and do nothing to make possible our young people's positive self-identity, I will be seen and judged by God. At the same time, doing something is a hard thing. Yet, I know that there is a God who wants us to know ourselves as valued even if there are humans who don't want us to and are working to assure that we don't know ourselves in this way. There's a lot that needs to be done in our schools to promote positive valuing of our heritage and our children's positive sense of self. I feel God is calling me to address this in the school where my children go. This is also an area where the church can get involved."

"The word *nigger* still stings deep in my soul. For Howard Thurman's grandmother to speak it aloud in order to affirm what we are *not* was tremendously motivating. She had to have known deep in her soul the meaning of Psalm 139. Anyway, I often hear that derogatory term from the lips of our young people, as though it were an affectionate term. That bothers me. I think one of the places both the Scripture and Grandmother's story is calling me to act is right where we live— in our homes, in our communities, and in our churches, to confront the use of the term there."

Activity 2—Decide Concrete Actions

In the final activity of the story-linking process, two sets of partners combine into a small group of four. In small groups, we decide specific responses to God's call to address negative self-identities and social contexts in which the responses will be made. We begin by answering the following questions: If you could fashion the most positive self-identity for African Americans of any age, what would it look like? What qualities would form a positive self-identity?

When these questions are answered, we brainstorm every context in which action is needed to liberate within persons in an ongoing way the positive self-identity we have described. The groups then choose one specific social context in which to design a programmatic response. Finally, the groups identify a specific kind of program and steps that their family or church can realistically undertake to accomplish the positive *self-identity* we have described. Groups also choose songs and scriptures that inspire action. Song examples include "You Are Near," which is a musical setting of Psalm 139,[6] and "This Little Light of Mine," which identifies the self as a light for Christ.[7] A scripture example is Matthew 5:14-16. The small group proposals are then shared with the total group.

Providing additional hints for addressing self-negating social contexts is a helpful follow-up to group proposals. Examples of such hints are as follows:

- Find another caring person to tell about experiences that threaten your positive self-identity. This can be someone in your family, church, school, community, or workplace. Moreover, be a caring other to someone else and help to form a caring network in your church or community.
- Cultivate a viable faith perspective. This means being aware of what we believe and have experienced about God through Jesus Christ in our lives. It also means taking note of our devotional practices—prayer and meditation, Bible study, and worship—wherein we are opened to God's presence and affirming activity in our lives.
- Identify with an exemplar of the Christian faith. Seek inspiration from and become a partner with a person in the Bible or in the Christian faith heritage who exemplifies what it means to form and act on positive self-identity.
- Keep alert to feelings of self-negation and image pathways to addressing positive self-identity in distressing social contexts.
- Become partners with others in envisioning ways of confronting self-negating social contexts and in acting to bring about affirming social contexts.

Follow-Up Suggestions

In a follow-up session, invite participants to share case illustrations, using fictitious names, of African Americans they know who are struggling to maintain positive identities in self-negating social contexts. Possible alternative scriptures for follow-up sessions include Genesis 16:1-6; 21:8-21; 2 Corinthians 5:17; Matthew 5:13-20; and Romans 8:12-18. These are scriptures that address identity struggles in difficult and oppressive contexts. An alternate approach to the African American Christian faith heritage story is to invite participants to share stories told by older members of their families that confront negative identities and seek to build positive ones.

The leader/teacher may also invite participants to share cultural sayings that focus on concerns for self and world. One such cultural saying is a commentary on the story of Hagar and Ishmael and refers to Hagar as "Aunt Haggie." The saying is presented in the discussion on Scripture in chapter 5.

CHAPTER 3

EXPLORING RELATIONSHIPS AND EVENTS OF OUR LIVES THROUGH STORY-LINKING

When there is that which I would claim as my very own, a second look, a sub-tle strangeness, something, announces that there can never be anything that is my very own. Always moving in upon life is the friend whose existence [we] did not know, whose coming and going is not [ours] to determine. . . . [Our] life is [our] very own and [our] life is never [ours] alone.

—Howard Thurman
The Inward Journey

Like the identities that are ours in the world we live in, our inter-personal relationships and life events are important interconnected dimensions of our everyday lives. Therefore, the story-linking process must rightly focus on relationships and life events. In this chap-ter, we will consider what they mean, what they have to do with liberat-ing wisdom, liberation and hope-filled vocation, and how they may be addressed in the story-linking process.

Interpersonal Relationships

Interpersonal relationships are the associations and connections we make with other people. We relate to family members, extended family, and friends. We have church, school, and work relationships. We relate in myriad ways to persons in other social and political institutions of the nation and with those whose religions and homelands reflect the global community in which we all live. Moreover, as Christians, we see ourselves in relationship with God through Jesus Christ. In all of these relationships, we hold various roles, behave in a variety of ways, and have particular views and feelings about these relationships.

We experience some relationships as liberating and some as stifling or paralyzing. We seek liberation from stifling or paralyzing relationships to significant, positive, and wholeness-producing ones; and our quest is for the wisdom to know what to do to make this happen. As Christians, we search for liberating wisdom from God, and we rely on Scripture and others whose faith has brought them through difficulty to show us the way. We also see our vocational role as that of Christ's helper in assuring and sustaining our own and others' liberation. In this role, we are also called to view those with whom we relate as creations of God, and to regard them as sisters and brothers.

We may say, "But this is so hard to do! Oppression seems to forever stalk and maim us! And even close relationships wound us!" Our purpose in this chapter is to consider our stories of relationships and to discover wisdom to foster liberating relationships in the midst of relational difficulties and a heart for vocation to make it happen for others. We will do this by reflecting critically on hard realities of relationships through use of additional case study material from Mary Johnson and Ken Brown. We will link with Scripture for its direction in liberating relationships and vocations that build hope in our own and others' relationships. We will also seek direction from an African American Christian faith heritage story.

Life Events

Life events include crises such as illness, hospitalization, disabling conditions, death, unfair treatment, broken relationships, job loss, homelessness, and incarceration. They also entail positive incidences such as gratifying memories, life-changing religious experiences, promotions, honors, mended relationships, and reunions. Life events also include incidents that mark stages of our lives, such as marriage, childbirth, school graduations, separation, divorce, becoming orphaned or widowed, and entering or exiting a chosen lifestyle or occupation.

Positive life events exhilarate us and free within us a sense of joy. Negative life events trouble us and sometimes bring us to the brink of spiritual and mental paralysis. Joyful events are worthy of celebration in community, and troubling events are needful of caring response by community members. When we celebrate together and care for one another, we are in hope-building vocation because, by our actions, we affirm and offer the promise of hope in persons' lives. For African Americans, this kind of vocation-centeredness builds on the historical-cultural view that is traceable to our African ancestry. The view is found in the African proverb "I am because we are, and since we are, therefore I am." A similar African proverb states, "One is only human because of others, with others, for others."

These wise proverbs highlight a "we" orientation to life and suggest that liberation and vocation evolve from communal awareness and demonstration of celebratory and caring kinship. In the early history of African Americans, the African ancestral "we" became connected with the Christian faith. It was informed by divine love attested to in Scripture and generated by an understanding of relationships based on communal love and caring. In the midst of oppressing events and suffering, persons experienced the transformed "we" as liberating. Celebration was possible in the "we" relationships. The "we" relationships freed people from hopelessness and the temptation to give up in the face of profoundly burdensome and painful life events. They were freed to develop a common vision of deliverance from oppressive forces, how to actualize that vision, and how to give support in the process. They were free to be in vocation.

As we enter the story-linking process in this chapter, we will keep alert to life events that call for celebration and those that call for caring response in the case studies and in our stories. Note the presence or absence of the African American "we" orientation. We will give attention to the nature of wisdom found in Scripture and in an African American Christian faith heritage story for what this wisdom nature tells us about liberating and vocation-centered responses to life events.

Phase One: Engage the Everyday Story

The following family stories of Mary Johnson and Ken Brown form the centerpiece for our entering the story-linking process in this chapter.

Focus here is on what the new case study material conveys about inter-personal relationships and life events.

Case Study 1: Mary Johnson's Family Story

Mary's family has come through many situations, but she quickly says:

> "We are still here. We've made it thus far by faith. And that's reason to celebrate. Of course it was hard for us when our daughter was diagnosed with cancer when she was an infant. But our family, friends, and the church we belonged to helped us get through that rough time. And, our daughter survived! It was hard, too, when my mother died some years ago. Then, after her death, a lot of care was needed for Dad. There were many trips across the country to look after him. After a number of years of gradually failing health, he died. The memory of both of them is dear even today—things like Mom's strength and the family history Dad passed on to us on tape.
>
> "There were any number of other problems and crises we've faced, too, from a son who didn't finish high school, worries about the safety of another son sent by the military to battle, and the pressures Bill faced on the job, to name a few. Life is full of surprises, some we would rather not receive; and when they come in bunches, sometimes it's hard to hang on. But you know, God has a way of giving us what we need to go on. This is the message I shared recently with a group of friends Bill and I invited to celebrate another year of my survival from breast cancer. More than that, we had recently become grandparents for the first time. It was important to rejoice at this miracle of life, too, especially since this grandbaby was born to our daughter who herself was the survivor of cancer in infancy."

Mary's words for what had happened in the family's life were: "It was like Christmas!" She continued:

> "I wanted family and friends to come together so that I could tell them, 'I have moved from fear to blessing.' When I was diagnosed with breast cancer, I was fearful of the road ahead—that my life was going to be cut short. But here I am! And, you can't imagine what it means, knowing our daughter lived beyond infancy, got through school, married, and is now a parent to our grandbaby.

"Honestly, I find myself asking daily, 'Why has God blessed me so?' I know others who are struggling with something major—whether it's a health problem, a job problem, a family problem, or you name it. And, I know from my work as a school teacher that many of our young are in troublesome situations at home and in school, not to mention in the community where so much is happening. Plus, we have only to look in the newspaper or see on the news some of the really tough battles we as African Americans continue to confront. But, again, my point is that I realize how blessed I am and, really, how blessed my family is. I am still alive! So is my daughter! And life goes on in the new generation begun in the birth of her child. We've come a long way together. And, we have a bigger family made up of many friends who have hung in there with us. Everybody doesn't have that. That weighs on my mind and my heart. What does all of this mean for me? Well, I really know it means that God has blessed me so I can be a blessing to someone else. I'm supposed to be there to help whoever I can."

Case Study 2: Ken Brown's Family Story

When sharing Ken Brown's story with a group I was guiding through the story-linking process, I mentioned that I had received a phone call asking prayer for Ken. One of the comments was: "Sometimes the stories of our lives leave a trail of tears that doesn't disappear. Deep hurt and sadness don't always get resolved and can haunt us in unforeseen ways. Maybe this is what happened to Ken." My questions to the group were "What clues do we see in Ken's story? What do we make of the following story of Ken's in our own lives and the lives of our families?"

"It's important that I tell it. I've come a long way in my twenty-five years. It reminds me of the road and new problems that are still ahead of me. I know there's no life without problems for me and others. I intend to help other people with theirs.

"Speaking of problems, I can still remember the morning my mom died. I was twelve years old. On that morning, I woke up to the sound of anguished cries, shouting, and moans. I knew what had happened. One of my sisters called 911. Two white paramedics came. They became frustrated by all of our crying, which got worse as they covered Mom and started to take her out. They gave us no comfort.

Maybe they weren't supposed to. They said to us very sharply and coldly, 'Shut up! Your crying won't do you any good!' Over the years, I've been able to overcome their treatment and insensitivity toward us. But it definitely was hard to take then.

"After Mom's death, I moved around a lot. I lived with foster parents. I lived for short periods with sisters and brothers in different cities. While I was with one of my brothers, I actually saw him shooting drugs. In fact, every one of my sisters and brothers had a problem with drugs or alcohol. One sister is struggling with that problem now and is a single parent with several children. One brother has since been incarcerated.

"I was put out of the home of one of my sisters during a difficult period when she and her husband were on drugs, and he was taking her money. I was fourteen then, and I lived on the streets. I didn't know anything to do but pray. I remembered that Mom always prayed, and she prayed for me before she died. I told God one day when I was lying on a bench in the rain that I knew the worst it could get was that I die, so let me die, or make it better. God and I had a good relationship; he helped me when things weren't going right. And God didn't foreclose on me. Time after time, God sent somebody. Someone intervened in my life at my most alienated moment.

"One time when I lived with my brother in another city, I enrolled in a middle school. Instead of being put in the eighth grade where I belonged, I was put in the sixth grade. I went to a magnet school while my mom was living and had managed to accomplish some things very well. So what happened just wasn't fair. Plus I was big for my age. I was embarrassed. I was ready to give up and drop out. I went to a white female counselor who asked me how I got behind. After hearing me read and watching me complete successfully the math problems she gave me, she took me to the black principal's office. He handed me a magazine, and I read it fluently. The counselor showed him my math work. I was then put in the seventh grade, and shortly after into the eighth-grade class. But I didn't stay in that school long. I moved in with my sister in another city.

"I enrolled in another school after moving. I had a report card from my previous school. With some testing, I went into the eighth grade. My teacher was very supportive. I worked hard. That teacher bought me a suit for my eighth-grade graduation. I moved to a children's home after graduation. I felt secure there. The executive director said that if I finished high school, she would help me get into college. The school got me tutors and even gave me guitar lessons. Well, I graduated, and the director saw that I entered college. I stopped college studies for a while, but went back after I got married. My wife became my greatest source of inspiration. She still is as I make my way through seminary.

"I know that God had a hand in my life. I often wonder what my life would be like if there hadn't been what I call miracles along the way. The help I've gotten from others has confirmed in my mind that there is a God who works through people to make us whole. I didn't always think this way. As a young kid, I really didn't believe God existed. I also had a lot of anger. Many times I bitterly thought, 'Why is life so hard? Why did Mom have to die?' She was a very good person. I wanted to know, 'Why were we treated so badly?' It occurs to me that maybe my brothers and sisters are struggling with these questions. Perhaps they haven't yet found a way to deal with what happened to Mom and to us when we were young.

"My constant prayer is that my brothers and sisters will somehow find a better way. I try to stay in contact with them. My oldest sister gave her life to Christ. I was recently with her when she had a serious operation. She is doing just fine. But there is a block between me and the others. They push me away because I'm a Christian and tell me they don't want to hear anything I have to say. It's very painful. They're my family, and they mean a lot to me. My greatest prayer is that they won't leave here before things are right between them and God and between them and me."

Activity 1—Disclose the Everyday Story

The new case material may be presented through prerecorded audiotapes using African American voices. It may also be read aloud by participants—a female for Mary Johnson's story and a male for Ken Brown's story, or the leader(s) may read it.

In an actual Christian education setting, I invite persons in advance of the case disclosures to listen for the nature of interpersonal relationships and life events, liberating wisdom, liberation and vocation that gives self and others a sense of hope. Participants are also invited to take note of what appears to be paralyzing roles, behaviors, and attitudes, and what in the stories calls for celebration and/or for caring response.

Activity 2—Critically Reflect on the Case Material

After the stories are presented, ask the participants to share their responses to the following questions:

- What relationships are positive and produce wholeness? In what ways?
- What relationships are stifling or paralyzing? How?
- What events call for celebration? Why?
- What events call for caring responses? Why?
- Where do you see evidence of liberating wisdom and experiences of liberation?
- Where do you see evidence of hope-centered vocation or blocks to it?

As indicated earlier, the strategy used for sharing depends on the group size and openness to sharing. In large groups, subgroups of three to four persons may be formed. They may report back upon conclusion of the sharing period. In situations where there is reticence of persons to share, I invite persons to choose a partner. After a period of partner sharing, two sets of partners may combine. A recorder from the group of four may then report the group's insights to the larger group.

Reflection Exercise

Reflect on what the case studies evoke in you and respond to the questions provided above. The following are responses given by actual participants:

Responses to Mary's Family Story

"Relationships were the mainstay in Mary's family. It is clear that she and her family were enabled to go through the trials and tribulations of their lives because they had a support network. She is right when she says that everybody doesn't have that."

"It's not easy to deal with death or the shadow of death. Those can be faith-testing times. We got a sense of Mary's awareness of God's blessing. How do you get past the doubt when things don't turn out the way they did for Mary and her family?"

"Mary's aware that other people struggle and that things don't turn out the same way for them. Her statement about being a blessing for others says that she doesn't take life for granted. That's liberating wisdom because she did not let the circumstances of her life bog her down. She saw something more for her life based on what she believed God had done in her life and her family's life. She really did have an understanding of vocation because she saw herself as a helper to others."

"Not knowing the outcome of a deadly disease can block us from moving on with our lives. Even though that wasn't the case with Mary, it happens."

Responses to Ken's Story

"Ken experienced some *big crises*. And, he bumped up against *big blocks* in relationships—the paramedics, school officials, and siblings. It would be easy for those two *bigs* to cause anyone to close everybody out, including God. But persons respond differently to crises and bad relationships. Ken always seemed ready to grab hold of liberating and caring relationships—memory of his mother's relationship with him, goodwilled school personnel, his wife. He did not let the blocking ones get him so far down that he couldn't get up. On the other hand, his brothers and sisters took a different approach. They created new crises for themselves through drugs and alcohol. For whatever reasons, they blocked their own liberation, vocation, and ability to enter into significant and meaningful 'we' relationships."

"The paramedics have no excuse for their bad attitudes. How they acted was stifling to the grief-stricken children. But just maybe they were freaked out because of seeing too much death. In any event, the children needed caring from someone. Then, too, they may not have been culturally sensitive."

"Because of the new and liberating relationships forged between key people and Ken, he was freed to get an education, to see the needs of others, and to respond to the vision God gave him for ministry. The church was not part of Ken's early relational network. But he does not say why. Is it possible that churches were blinded to what liberation and vocation meant for those in Ken's neighborhood?"

"We can only guess that whatever Ken's situation is now—whatever struggles he's going through—his past plays a part in it. It's hard to overcome some of the bad 'stuff' that happens to us. It can haunt us and even come back in new ways and situations. The truth is, we can choose how to deal with where we've been and where we are now. Maybe Ken's struggling with choices."

Phase Two: Engage the Christian Faith Story in the Bible

Phase two of the story-linking process is concerned with linking case material and participant reflections with Scripture. What guidance does Scripture give about interpersonal relationships and life events? By way of illustration, Mark 2:1-12, the story of the paralytic, will be used. This story holds particular significance in terms of interpersonal relationships and life events of African Americans.

The story contains liberating wisdom and mirrors meanings of liberating relationships and hope-building vocation. It reveals a relational "we" response in the life of one who, like African Americans, experienced a traumatic life event, oppressive circumstances, and a difficult situation of isolation. This story allows us to identify with the role of the paralytic and to imagine our living out his liberating story. But it also allows us to see ourselves in liberating and vocation-centered relationships through our imaginative engagement in the role of the helpers in the story. Moreover, it fosters re-imaging our relationship with God through Jesus Christ and the liberation and hope-centered vocation that is energized in that relationship.

Activity 1—Disclose the Bible Story/Text

I invite persons to enter the story found in Acts 27:1-44 of the apostle Paul's dramatic journey to Rome, the city of his destiny.[1] I introduce the scripture as a story told by a narrator about the wisdom shown by Paul and the help of an unsuspecting other in a life-threatening situation as he and some fellow prisoners were being transferred by ship from one location to another. It is a story of bold courage under fire and faith in God's presence and activity on a voyage that could have ended far differently than it did. I then indicate that we will have three readings of the story. The first reading takes place in this first activity. This reading, guided by the following questions, is done individually and silently.

- What happens in the unfolding scenes of the story that signals trouble?
- What becomes Paul's role in the unfolding story, and why is it needed?
- What was the nature of Paul's wisdom in the unfolding story? Who else demonstrated wise action?
- How was Paul's wisdom received? What behaviors and attitudes were exhibited by others around Paul? What and when do questions about hope emerge?
- What was Paul facing beyond the current situation? Knowing what is ahead of him, why wouldn't he simply give up and allow the present situation to come to a disastrous end?
- What words or phrases of Paul's "stick out" as reflections of liberating wisdom?
- How does the story demonstrate meanings of liberation? Hope-building vocation?

Responses to some of the questions are addressed in Activity 2.

Activity 2—Focus on the Bible Story as Mirror

In activity 2, I invite small groups of three or four persons to explore the story together in order to get an internal "picture" of the unfolding story. Afterward, to further assist the participants' grasp of the story, they respond within the whole group setting to the guiding questions posed in activity 1. To assist this response, the questions are repeated.

Reflection Exercise

Read the story of the apostle Paul's journey found in Acts 27:1-44. Consider your answers to the questions raised above. Some responses given by actual participants are as follows:

"The most telling part of the story is Paul's stepping forward and unashamedly and unapologetically taking charge of the situation even though he was a prisoner. That reminds me of a saying I learned from my grandmother: 'A prison cell does not a prisoner make.' Paul obviously felt free to act because he knew who and Whose he was. And, he knew that the very lives of everybody on board were at stake."

"Paul knew what he had to do and knew how to do it. He didn't rely on his own understanding. He relied on God. A powerful statement of liberating wisdom came from the angel who appeared to him and assured him that all would have safe passage. But Paul's wisdom came through one of his statements to the others to keep up their courage, and in another statement: 'Stay in the ship.'"

"In the end, everyone was delivered from the storm. But it did not happen solely on Paul's individual effort. He knew God would not foreclose on him. Also, Julius the Centurion came through as an all-right guy as well. It was not a whole community effort. But it turned out to be more than just Paul's wisdom alone. Vocation gets carried out in unsuspecting ways for God's purposes."

"Something happened when Paul gathered everyone together for food. Paul and Julius had *courage*. And the rest became *encouraged* when they came together and had what looked like communion. Still, Paul and the other prisoners could have been killed after this high moment of unity and gratitude if it had not been for Julius."

Activity 3—Enter as Partner with the Bible Story Actors

In activity 3, participants engage in a role-play of the story of Paul's treacherous journey at sea. Volunteers are invited to take the following roles: Paul, several other prisoners, Julius, several other soldiers, the pilot of the ship, and the angel of God. I invite remaining participants to create the sound effects of the storm. I encourage the actors to get in touch with what is happening to them as they act out their roles. They are to give attention to their feelings about themselves and what happens to them as they "live" the story. Time is also given for the actors to review the story and to identify story lines that they want to include or read verbatim from the Bible.

At the close of the role-play, participants are invited to respond to the guiding question: What thoughts and feelings did the role-play evoke in you?

Reflection Exercise

Image yourself as Paul in the story. Then image yourself as one or more of the other persons in the story. Based on your imaging, respond to the above question.

Some responses given by actual participants are as follows:

"In my role as Paul, I felt myself become energized. A new sense of courage came upon me. I was surprised by the help Julius gave me, but was grateful for it. It was assurance that God 'had my back.'"

"Even though I was one of the soldiers in authority, I lost that authority because of my fear. It came to me that Paul knew more than I did about sailing. I did not want to die."

"As I acted out Julius's part, I became aware that, actually, I came to a point where I was 'sticking my neck out' and might later receive a reprimand for it. But I felt compelled to treat Paul kindly and to save him, even though I wasn't sure why."

"My role as an angel drove home to me the idea of God's presence and action in that situation."

Activity 4—Envision God's Activity Today

Activity 4 helps identify where God is at work among African Americans today. How is God's liberating wisdom revealed to us in the midst of the storms of our lives? How is God bringing about our deliverance from the devastating consequences of those storms? Who and what is the nature of another's vocation that gives us hope and helps through the storms? What kinds of relational support and hope-building vocation do we demonstrate for the sake of others' liberation?

I invite participants to choose partners. With their partners, they recall one specific person whom they feel God sent to care for them during a tough time in their lives. They recall the name of the person, what the person looks like, and their relationships to that person. They recall when and how the person showed caring. And they recall how they felt about this relationship.

I also invite participants to recall in the presence of their partners an instance when they felt God called them to be positive and caring helpers for another person in a difficult circumstance. They recall the name of the person, what the person looked like, and their relationship to the person. They recall the circumstance under which they felt called to help. And they recall how they felt about this relationship.

Participants are then invited to recall a tough situation when they felt God's activity in an unmistakable way. They recall the situation and what made it a tough one. They recall how God acted in the unfolding of that situation.

Reflection Exercise

Reflect on your own story of struggle in a tough or crisis situation, using the above format.

Activity 5—Anticipate Ongoing Response to God

In this period of sharing, two sets of partners combine to identify where God is now calling for caring responses. Particular attention is given to troubling relationships or tough life events. We call to mind relationships and life events of which we are aware—in families, work, school, church, community, and other places—that are experienced as storms that threaten to "shipwreck" our lives. We then list them on newsprint or tablet for use in the final phase of the story-linking process. Examples of responses on newsprint or tablet have typically included:

Family: Help for parents relating to children who act out; response to teens' need for parental presence; care for an elderly parent whose health is declining and who resists help, and how to balance care for others with self-care and need for "time out."

Work: Experience of job layoff, insufficient benefits, inability in finding other employment, and dealing with an uncertain future.

School: Fear of unpopularity, concern for violence, and experience of negative regard and racist comments by white teachers toward African Americans.

Church: An "in-group" attitude that excludes and belittles newcomers or those who are considered different or from the "wrong side."

Community: Unrelenting racial profiling and instances of brutality, continuing struggles for safe neighborhoods including safety from violence and environmental safeguards, and fair and respectful treatment in public life.

Reflection Exercise

What troubling or potential "shipwreck"-producing relationships or life events are in need of caring response in your work, school, church, or community?

Phase Three: Engage a Christian Faith Story from the African-American Heritage

How did our forebears confront troubling or potential "shipwreck"-producing relationships and life events? An important story to illustrate this phase of the story-linking process is that of Josiah Henson.[2] His story tells of a man and his family who experienced the solidarity of family amid the brutality of slavery. In this story, we become privy to the enlivening presence of God in the lives of persons whose relationships and life events would be considered by most to be dead-end or most certainly "shipwrecked." We discover a man who saw a "we" orientation as the only way to show Christian caring.

Activity 1—Disclose the Faith Heritage Story

I invite persons to glean as much as they can about the nature of relationships and life events, and how they are dealt with in the Josiah Henson story. The story may be presented on prerecorded audiotape using one African American voice for the narrator portions. An African American male voice should be used where Henson's first-person words appear. An African American female's voice should be used where Mother Henson's words appear. Participants may also present the story as indicated below:

> **Narrator:** Josiah Henson was born a slave in 1789. His first recollection was of his father's severe beating because his father had come to the defense of Josiah's mother, who was being accosted by the slave overseer. Josiah described seeing the penalty being meted out.

> **Josiah:** The penalty was one hundred lashes on his bare back, and his right ear nailed to the whipping post, and then severed from his body.

Narrator: Josiah's father was later sent from the state of Maryland (where this happened) to Alabama. Josiah's mother and six children remained on the estate. He thought of her:

Josiah: She was a good mother to us, a woman of deep piety, anxious above all things to touch our hearts with a sense of religion. I don't know how or where she acquired her acquaintance with the Lord's Prayer, which she so frequently taught us to repeat. . . . I remember seeing her often on her knees, trying to arrange her thoughts in prayer appropriate to her situation. . . . and which have remained in my memory to this hour. . . . We were but property—not a mother and children God had given her.

Narrator: And Josiah remembered that because of the reality that they were property, the children were eventually sold, one by one, away from their mother and then she was sold. Josiah was about five or six years old when this happened. He recalled his mother pleading for her children, only to be kicked away.

Josiah: I saw the groan of her suffering body and the sob of her breaking heart. I heard her cry out:

Mother: Oh, Lord Jesus, how long, how long shall I suffer this way?

Narrator: Throughout his early years as a slave, Josiah was oppressed by his circumstances and oppressed "with a load of sorrow" for the male slaves' condition, which was bad enough, but more particularly for the slave women's suffering. He felt driven to do whatever he could for them in a clandestine way.

At eighteen years old, Josiah came to believe that he had a responsibility to God. He had sneaked away to hear a sermon at the risk of being caught and beaten. He heard the scriptural passage of Hebrews 2:19, which told that God, through Christ, tasted death for *everyone*. For the first time, he felt the confirmation of a Supreme Being who had compassion for *all*, including him and others living under the sting of oppression. Josiah found himself saying:

Josiah: Jesus will be my dear refuge—he'll wipe away all tears from my eyes. Now I can bear all things; nothing will seem hard after this.

Narrator: He described this as his conversion, or the awakening of a new life—a consciousness of a new power and destiny. Josiah's suffering in the throes of slavery continued, but he also continued to do whatever he could for others who shared the same miserable condition. He married a slave girl. They had twelve children, eight of whom survived childhood. He admits to acting out of ignorance on some occasions. He did not apologize for his feeling of hatred of the system and bitterness toward those in the system who often promised one thing and did another. He became absorbed with the quest of his soul for freedom and self-assertion. For he said:

Josiah: I am ready and willing to pray and to put forth vigorous action.

Narrator: At one point Josiah gained his freedom and a certificate showing it, only to find himself tricked out of them and pushed to be wholly reliant on God. At another point, he was taken away from his wife and children.

Josiah: I was placed in a "slave-pen." I felt sure I'd die.

Narrator: Josiah contemplated murder as a means of ensuring his escape. But he could not go through with it. He said:

Josiah: To murder would destroy my own character, the value of life and my peace of mind.

Narrator: Still, he was reunited with his wife and two children and, together, they were able to escape to freedom. They reached Cincinnati, Ohio, and were able to get the comfort of rest and shelter from good Samaritans. After resting, they headed on through the wilderness. They happened onto an Indian encampment and received hospitality from the Indians. They finally knew they were delivered when they were picked up by a boat. This was 1830. Josiah described it:

Josiah: My black friend and two sailors jumped out. . . . Three hearty cheers welcomed us as we reached the schooner, and never till my dying shall I forget the shout of the captain: "Come up on deck and clap your wings and crow like a rooster. You're free."

Narrator: You can imagine Josiah's joy.

Josiah: I threw myself on the ground, rolled in the sand, seized handfuls of it and kissed them, and danced round till, in the eyes of several who were present, I passed for a madman.

Narrator: Josiah became a preacher. As his eldest boy learned to read in school, he taught Josiah to read. Josiah saw that there was room for betterment in the conditions of the blacks in the place where they settled. He also felt that none of them should be content with the first joy of their deliverance. Josiah insisted that they needed to become of one mind for their betterment. And Josiah himself felt called to work for the liberation of brothers and sisters still in slavery. He said:

Josiah: After I had tasted the blessings of freedom, my mind reverted to those who I knew were groaning in captivity, and I at once proceeded to take measures to free as many as I could. I thought that by using exertion, numbers might make their escape as I did, if they had some practical advice how to proceed.

Narrator: Moreover, in his preaching, Josiah tried to impress upon other blacks who had tasted freedom something else about their obligations. He said:

Josiah: We are obligated first to God, for our deliverance; and then, second, to our fellow sojourners, to do all that is in our power to bring others out of bondage.

Activity 2—Describe the Liberating Wisdom, Liberation Mind-Set, and Liberation and Vocational Strategies

Participants share their observations of relationships and life events, and how these were dealt with in the story. In particular, group members are asked to look for the wisdom conveyed by Josiah Henson, for a communal liberation mind-set in the story and for a "we" strategy in addressing the storms of life that had the potential of irreversibly "shipwrecking" his and others' lives. The guiding questions are:

• What evidence did you see of Josiah Henson's unwavering focus on liberation for him, his family, and others?

- What were some instances when liberating wisdom emerged? What was the nature of the wisdom?
- Why didn't he give up? Where and how was hope stirred by his understanding of vocation?
- Where in his story did a "we" strategy appear?
- How would you compare his story to the story of Paul's journey through the storm at sea found in Acts 27?
- What qualities in the Josiah Henson story would you like to emulate? Why?
- What qualities would you like to see emulated in your congregation?

Reflection Exercise

What answers would you give to the questions? Responses of actual participants include:

"The family unit was important to Josiah and freedom for all of them, not just for himself, was pivotal. But it was clear that he had a commitment to the liberation of 'fellow sojourners.' In these ways, his strategy was definitely 'we' oriented."

"He had a real relationship with God, and that relationship propelled him forward to help others no matter what. He had reverence for the life of all. He chose to take the opportunities that came as he saw them rather than to murder."

"Our family members need Josiah's and his family's mind-set."

"Our congregations—each one of us— need the communal commitment that Josiah had. We also need to be willing to admit, as he did, that we don't always have the answers and we may make some ignorant moves along the way. Yet, together, we can make it."

Phase Four: Engage in Christian Ethical Decision Making

The intent in the final phase of the story-linking process is to guide persons toward deciding action. We give particular attention to what

God is calling us to do to respond to the troubling relationships and events listed on newsprint or tablet by the groups earlier in the story-linking process. We are also to decide ways to celebrate positive relations and events.

Activity 1—Discern God's Call

The groups begin by reviewing the list of troubling relationships and events they listed on the newsprint or tablet in phase two. The groups are then invited to engage in a "silent memory summation" of the story of the apostle Paul's harrowing journey at sea and the Josiah Henson story. In this summation exercise, group members call to mind two or three examples of liberating wisdom that struck them as being important in averting a self-defeating life direction, or a life journey likened to a "shipwreck."

Group members also call to mind two or three relational qualities in the stories that struck them as being important to a communal or positive relational mind-set. These qualities become a starting point for the groups' describing the kind of communal mind-set needed to address the troubling relationships and life events they listed earlier on newsprint or tablet. Participants are guided by the question: What are the qualities— including attitudes, ideas, and approaches—needed to carry out caring responses to troubling relationships and events in each participant's family, work, school, church, and community?

Reflection Exercise

Enter into a time of silent memory summation. Then say something about the liberating wisdom you gleaned from the stories of the apostle Paul and Josiah Henson. Also describe the communal mind-set you would seek to carry out in tough circumstances in your own life or on behalf of others.

Responses of actual participants include:

> "I want to hold always in my heart and act on the words of the apostle Paul: 'Keep up your courage. . . . I have faith in God. . . . Unless [you] stay in the ship, you cannot be saved.' Those words ring out as liberating wisdom for going through the storms of life, whether they take the form of difficult relationships or life events that test us on every side."

"The liberating wisdom that stuck out for me was Josiah Henson's statement that we are obligated to God for our deliverance. That comes first. And, then, we are compelled to do all we can on behalf of others' rescue from whatever binds them."

"Not leaving others behind, but at the same time acknowledging when we need help and seeking to help one another is important."

"Taking the time to show caring and making a commitment to give back to community are at the center of a communal mind-set."

Activity 2—Decide on Concrete Actions

In the final activity, persons decide how and when to respond to God's call to address troubling relationships and life events. From the newsprint or tablet list, the group designates one troubling relationship or life event as highest priority. The groups brainstorm all possible actions they, family members, and their congregation can take that hold realistic potential for positive response. From the options, they choose one action for themselves, one for identified family members, and one for the congregation as extended family. They then develop specific approaches and a timeline to accomplish the actions. Examples of suggested actions include the following:

- Form a "Hope-Builders Circle for Parents" that would establish regular meetings to receive from knowledgeable advisers and from one another wisdom for positive and effective parenting.
- Form a "You and Your Aging Parent" workshop with leaders who can provide advice on caring for aging relatives.
- Develop intentional family times for family communication and seek guidance from professionals when needed.
- Create a job bank with lists of available jobs in the community and persons who can assist in application and interview preparation.
- Initiate an "Adopt a School" program in the congregation.
- Hold an open church forum on what it means to be a welcoming congregation. Volunteer to be greeters for new visitors to church services.
- Establish neighborhood watch groups to monitor community safety and environmental issues and not simply suggest but act on plans for addressing the issues.

Finally, the small groups decide a way of celebrating their group relationship that can be carried out as a culminating celebratory activity and used in other places such as the family, church event, or community setting. Ideas include writing a litany, poem, or rap; celebrating through song and/or movement; planning and carrying out a "Welcome Table" meal of food and recipes brought by each person. The small groups then share their decisions with the whole group and settle on whole-group participation in instances that would allow for entire group celebration.

Follow-Up Suggestions

Develop your own everyday case studies on interpersonal relationships and life events or ask group participants to do so. The following alternative Bible passages may be used in follow-up sessions: Psalms 13; 33:13-22; Romans 12:9-13; 13:8-10; Mark 2:1-12. For persons who are struggling with difficult relationships and life events, Psalm 13 offers an avenue for voicing and reflecting openly on anguish. This psalm should be presented, however, with Psalm 33:13-22. The latter text allows persons to identify with the theme of promise. The passage from Romans is helpful because of its focus on qualities that characterize liberating and hope-building vocation. Also, central to this passage is a "we" orientation. The story of the paralytic in the Markan passage invites reflection on how we are enabled to move through paralyzing circumstances in our lives.

The story of Irene McCoy Gaines is an alternate African American Christian faith heritage story that also presents liberating wisdom and "pictures" of liberating and hope-building vocational action in the throes of difficult relationships and life events. Out of her struggles as an African American woman, Ms. Gaines became a civil rights activist, civic worker, social worker, and advocate on behalf of African Americans. Her story is found in *Notable Black American Women*, edited by Jessie Carney Smith.[3]

Sermon material may also be substituted in the heritage story phase. For example, the sermon by H. Beecher Hicks Jr. titled "I've Been in the Storm So Long," found in *Preaching Through a Storm*, addresses the theme of triumph out of anguish.[4] Moreover, testimony songs such as "I Don't Feel No Ways Tired," or prayer songs such as "When the Storms of Life Are Raging, Stand by Me,"[5] may also be used to append the heritage story phase or to conclude the story-linking process.[6]

CHAPTER 4

EXPLORING LIFE MEANINGS THROUGH STORY-LINKING

It is ever a grace and a benediction to be able to come to a halt . . . to turn aside from the things that occupy and preoccupy our minds in the daily round, to take a long intimate look at ourselves both retrospect and prospect. . . . It is at such times that we are free to remember! From within the quiet of our spirits we may see with startling clarity the meaning of past experiences.

—Howard Thurman
The Inward Journey

Assigning meaning to our experiences is a natural and important way of making sense of life. In meaning-making, we ponder and judge all that makes up our lives—our identities, social contexts, interpersonal relationships, and life events. Our meaning-making is our attempt to bring order and purpose in our lives. Meaning-making is our way of saying, "This is how I see life and my place in it, and this is what I'm going to do about it." How we fill in and act on the details contributes to our story plot. And how our story plot unfolds contributes to our ongoing meaning-making. So, life meanings and story plots are very much related.

We assign meanings to the happenings of our lives and arrive at various degrees of understanding of our purposes, and we have a great deal to say about how our plots unfold. Indeed, we have a lot to say about whether our unfolding plots will be liberating or blocking for us and others, and whether they do or do not reflect our being in the kind of vocation that is hope-building for us and others.

When we become Christians, we choose a Christian story plot. We see life through the eyes of God made known in Jesus Christ. Our being in life is seen as a gift, as valuable, and as having promise even in the midst of trial and tribulation. We choose to be linked with and set our life direction after the Example and Source of a liberating plot. Our unfolding plot becomes defined by hope-filled purpose, based on God's ongoing value of us and expectation of our valuing others. It becomes defined by care and concern that extends beyond self to others. We see our purpose in vocational terms and as a calling from God.

Someone is apt to say, "Hold it! Not so fast! It's not that easy!" And we know these thoughts sometimes come. When we are assailed by ongoing racial discrimination and other trials and tribulations, there is the temptation to succumb to an approach to life that says, "Life is a horrid mistake." Or "Life is a barrel of lemons out of which no lemonade can possibly be made." But the nature of vocation as calling demands that we find and choose those ways wherein Christ becomes present through each one of us. We choose to continue to reach out, hold, sustain, and advocate on behalf of one another until any block to liberation for us and others is dismantled. How is this possible?

In this chapter, we will engage in a story-linking process focused on life meanings and story plots. We will consider whether our story plots are liberating and whether they contain a sense of vocation and positive life meaning from the Christian viewpoint. Likewise, we will consider hindrances to living the Christian story plot and arriving at positive life meanings based on this plot. We want to become alert to judgments we have of our stories as dissatisfying, futile, or meaningless; and we want to explore the nature of liberating wisdom that can help to reorient such stories toward positive life meanings. The case studies of Mary Johnson's family and Ken Brown's family will continue as means of entering the story-linking process focused on life meanings.

Phase One: Engage the Everyday Story

The following case material reveals aspects of the themes of identity, social contexts, interpersonal relationships, and life events found in the family stories of Mary Johnson and Ken Brown. However, we will focus expressly on meanings each of these individuals assigns to their lives and on the nature of their story plots.

Case Study 1: Mary Johnson's Story

Mary Johnson recalled parts of the twists and turns in her unfolding story shared a while ago:

"My life has been no bed of roses. But I'd guess you could say that about most, if not all, of us. Do you know anyone who has lived a perfect, trouble-free life? I surely don't, although I'm sure some have had a worse time of it than I, judging from what I know about real hardship cases abuse, you name it—told by our young in the school where I teach. Sometimes it's hard to be optimistic about life, but I do look at myself pretty much as an optimist. Basically, I believe you can't give up on life. If you're going to get anything out of life, somehow you're going to have to hang in there. Still, I confess there have been times when I was guilty of throwing my hands up and, for a time, sitting down on life.

"I recall when our family was uprooted because of my husband's job situation. As a result, we got into some marital difficulty. It was hard on the children. And, the church we thought was going to be supportive and a good place for the children turned out differently. It was not a welcoming place. Instead, it was alienating. At that point, my life just stalled.

"As I said sometime ago, I felt like I was doomed. Although I had been a teacher and had enjoyed teaching, I couldn't seem to get started again. The children were having a hard time, too. I could see that. But I was at a loss to do anything about it. I became a totally dependent person without a life of my own and no financial resources of my own. I hit bottom.

"The New Year's Eve service I attended at a church other than the one I mentioned earlier was a turning point in my life. I owe where I am today largely to what happened at that service. During the last part of the service, those attending were asked to write a letter to God about how we felt about our lives. We were to confess to God what we had not done for ourselves and others that we could and should have done as responsible Christians. We were to tell God what we intended to do in the New Year. And we were to ask for and cooperate with God's guidance.

"I poured out to God all I could in the time we had to write the letter—my inadequate feelings, my feelings that my life had gone 'down the drain,' my disappointment in myself and in my church. I wrote that I was going to live my life differently in the New Year. I wrote that I had abilities I had laid aside. I wrote that I would seek certification for teaching. I also said that I would not keep quiet about the church's alienating atmosphere since I knew it was affecting others. And I committed to daily prayer. When we finished, we were told to put the letters in an envelope we had been given. We sealed the envelopes, addressed them to ourselves, and placed them at the altar during Communion. We were told the envelopes would be mailed to us at year's end.

"Over the year, I found myself being guided and empowered by God. I enrolled in school to get teacher certification. I applied for and got a position as a teaching assistant. I spoke to church leaders about the alienating atmosphere, and it became an important item for discussion and action. I faithfully prayed every day. My life definitely moved in a different direction. I got the letter back at the end of the year. I saw how important it is not to give up on life or on myself.

"Now, I can say that I think what happened to me during that New Year's Eve service had a big effect on my life right up to now. And, I think what happened to me had an impact on my family. I later became a full-time certified classroom teacher, and I returned to school for a graduate degree. Our family grew closer together. The children have done all right for themselves. Of course there were struggles along with the triumphs—times when, in their teen years, my children and I didn't see eye to eye and when their getting an award or certificate brought tears to my eyes. I keep wondering, though, what might have been done differently with the one who did not finish high school; but, still, there have been no really difficult problems. I am grateful for that.

"What's my approach to life? Remember now, I'm a cancer survivor. God has brought me this far by faith; and God has something more for me to do. I said that I'm an optimist. But that doesn't say it all. I'll say it again and again: 'I'm blessed and I'm here to be a blessing to others.'"

Case Study 2: Ken Brown's Story

Ken Brown had shared much about his life that concluded with the phone call from a friend requesting prayer for him. Ken continued his story by saying:

> "It is difficult to think of my life without thinking about the lives of those I grew up with and where I grew up—my brothers and sisters, neighbors, dilapidated apartments and houses, tight spaces, not much to live on, gangs, drugs. You see, I was able somehow to find a way out. But for most of the others, nothing has changed except a new generation growing up in the same place in the same way. I'll have to admit, a big part of me—my heart—is still there. When I think of all that needs to be done in that place and in places like it all over the country . . . [Ken's voice trailed off.]
>
> "So, when I think about meaning in life, it's hard for me to separate meaning as far as I'm concerned and meaning as far as those I grew up with are concerned. Yes, I've heard people say life is what you make it, and there's some truth in that. But people get to where they are for many reasons—some by their own doing, some because of tough breaks in life, and some because they were born into it. But I have seen what the conditions of poor people can do to you. My mother and many others like her had a lot of pride. She and a lot of others did everything they could that's honest and decent to make a decent life where, in a lot of ways, there was little that made for real living in terms of the things they needed to survive. I know that hasn't changed for a whole lot of folk. It's often a real fight for them to hold their heads up.
>
> "Many outside the neighborhood were, frankly, unfriendly, insensitive, and discouraging. I told you earlier about the unkind paramedics. That is only the tip of the iceberg when it comes to how people in our neighborhood are treated by public agencies and officials who are supposed to care. Churches are not always that much different either. Also, slumlords are for real. There's only so much that you can fix up or patch up. After a while, people just give up. You've heard that old saying 'You can't fight city hall.' Well, when you're poor, you feel like for sure you can't, so what happens is that a lot of 'kicking one another' goes on inside the neighborhood. It's a way of kicking at whatever reminds you of your own inadequacy, inferiority, and humiliation. Even though it's not a good way to deal with

the raw deals life gives you, it happens nonetheless. When people feel defeated, well . . . [Ken's voice trailed off.]

"I ran across a book one time called *Growing Up Absurd* [by Paul Goodman] that said when people do not see anything worthwhile, they cannot do anything worthwhile. They begin to feel like their lives are starved. And when their lives are starved, they begin to ask the question 'Am I nothing?' That's what life means to a lot of people I know. I know that's the case with the homeless people who come to the soup kitchen where I currently volunteer. It's the case with some youth I am working with. That has to change. In order for my life to have meaning, I feel I've got to do something to help change things. I know that's what I've been called to do."

Activity 1—Disclose the Everyday Story

As suggested previously, the case study material may be presented through prerecorded audiotape using African American voices. Or it may be read aloud by participants—a female for Mary's story and a male for Ken's story. Or the material may be read aloud to the participants by the leader(s)/teacher(s).

In an actual Christian education setting, I invite persons in advance of the case disclosures to listen with the following questions in mind:

- Do Mary and Ken link with a liberating plot and, if so, what is that plot?
- Do Mary and Ken have an overall sense of hopefulness and purpose in life that is liberating for them and potentially liberating for others? Where do they display liberating wisdom?
- Is there anything in their stories that conveys they have dealt with positive and negative meanings in life? If so, where and how did they do it?
- How do you feel about Mary's and Ken's views about life, and what questions do their stories raise? What memories and issues do their stories raise for you?

Activity 2—Critically Reflect on the Case Material

I repeat the questions raised prior to the case disclosures and invite participants to share their responses.

Reflection Exercise

What answers would you give to the questions posed above? The following are responses given by actual participants:

Reflections on Mary Johnson's Meaning-Making

"Mary says she looks at life optimistically. That's the main theme or plot to her story. But she also seems to look at life realistically. Life isn't a bed of roses. Life is hard. But given that reality, Mary doesn't stay down when she gets down. That's a plus in terms of making any kind of sense and meaning out of life."

"She's also a risk-taker. She went to another church and responded to something she saw as useful. It sounds like she went looking for her liberation and vocation. She went back to her own church to 'blow the whistle.' That took courage, and by doing what she did, she helped free them to a better kind of vocation. Plus it made her feel better about her own life."

"Her story puts us on notice that meaning in life doesn't come by sitting still. People can't sit still and let life run over them if they expect to contribute something to life and get something out of life."

"Mary also showed that you can get energized when you're in touch with God. She showed that Christians can find purpose and exercise purpose when they're in touch with God. That's the only way to make sense of life."

"Mary's on track in terms of vocation. She stopped resisting her calling to teach. But her story raises the issue for a lot of people, including some of us, that we do resist what God is calling us to do and then we wonder why we have a problem with meaning in life."

"Having a life-threatening illness seems to have given Mary an extra measure of wisdom and a special outlook on her life and how she will live it. Her view of vocation as blessing others is special."

Reflections on Ken Brown's Meaning-Making

"It must have been difficult for Ken to come out on the positive side. He seems to have done it in terms of what he shared. I wonder if the phone call was a signal that his battle with his past really isn't over."

"Ken sure hits us with our responsibility to minister to others so that they can find hope and positive meaning in their lives. Really, he's convicted many of us. On the other hand, how far can we go in taking responsibility? Yet, when we look at Ken's brothers and sisters, how much can Ken or we do for someone who doesn't seem to want help or doesn't seem to help themselves? Questions about how hard to try, plus not knowing exactly what to do, can block our vocation, their liberation, and our meaning in life. At the same time, we ought not use that as an excuse to cop out of our responsibility to be in vocation, because if we do, we've failed our calling to vocation."

"Hope? Ken seemed to have it, and his sense of vocational aspirations showed it. I just pray that he's anchored enough in his faith to be able to hold on to it. In situations like his, it's probably a tricky thing."

Activity 3—Identity with the Case Study

Following critical reflection on the case studies, I invite participants to share with a partner or in small groups what the case material evoked in them about their own meaning-making. Starter questions include:

- To what extent did you see your own plot or generating theme in Mary's and Ken's stories?
- Is the way you look at life and go about life similar to or different from Mary and Ken? How?
- What impact does life outlook have on your sense of being liberated and being in vocation? What impact does it have on life meaning for you? What is the place of hope?
- What words or phrases would you use to describe the plot or generating theme of your story?

Responses to the questions are then shared in the large group.

Reflection Exercise

Reflect on your life meaning in light of Mary's and Ken's stories. How would you answer the questions posed above?

I have found that some persons more closely identify with what Mary had to say than with Ken's statements—while, for others, it is just the reverse. There are also those who say that what Mary or Ken shared could very well have been their own story. A few also respond to Mary's story by focusing on Mary's children, especially the son who didn't finish high school; or to Ken's story by focusing on Ken's siblings. In comparing their own stories with Mary's, Ken's, or family members' in their stories, persons find clear points of similarity and of differentiation. Some also share the difficulties they have in coming to positive life meaning. It is important that the leader/teacher guide the group to avoid "getting stuck" at this point. This may be done by encouraging them to stay with the story-linking process and to see what the rest of the process has to say to them.

Phase Two: Engage the Christian Faith Story in the Bible

In phase two, we link our reflections on Mary's, Ken's, and our own stories with Scripture. The question is: What does Scripture have to say about life meaning? The following illustrates an approach to answering the question.

Helpful passages are Hebrews 10:39; 11:1-40; and 12:1-2. This particular passage is helpful to an African American discussion of life meaning because it reveals a message about the meaning of life amid adversity and oppression on which African Americans, past and present, have relied. In fact, in African American church settings, the "Honor Roll of the Faithful," which appears in chapter 11 of Hebrews, is often appended to include an Honor Roll of African Americans who have kept the faith.

In the passage from Hebrews, we find faith as the major theme. The author was responding to early Christians who were discouraged and had lost hope and meaning due to the perils of life, harassment, and oppression. The scripture witnesses to what it means to seek, find, and refuse to relinquish faith that brings positive life meaning in the midst of trial and tribulation.

The Scripture provides for African Americans a litany of God's relationship with another people. It evokes our telling of God's acting in our own history. It reveals a perspective of faith and hope in God's

ongoing relationship with us and God's desire for our liberation, vocation, and life meaning. Indeed, it challenges us to reflect on our faith in
God's activity, on our response to God's Word in whatever situation we
find ourselves today, and on the relation of these to our meaning-making.[1]

Activity 1—Disclose the Bible Story

I invite persons to enter the passages from Hebrews. I introduce the
scripture by saying that it tells the story of a writer's response to early
Christians who lived in a place called the Lycus Valley. They were discouraged and confronted doubts, hopelessness, and weakening faith due
to adversity and oppression. Participants are then invited into two readings of the scripture. First, they read the passage alone silently, or they
read the verses alternately with a partner. Second, the whole group enters
into a choral reading of the scripture.

In advance of the choral reading, I provide questions to consider,
including:

- What was the plot or generating theme in the scripture? What
  words or phrases convey the plot? Would you describe the plot
  as liberating? Why?
- Would you say that those on the "Honor Roll of Faith" were in
  hope-building vocation? Why? What meanings did life have
  for them?
- Where do you find wisdom in the scripture that is particularly
  helpful to you?
- In what ways does the scripture challenge your approach to life
  and meaning-making today?

It is helpful to explain that a choral reading involves solo and unison
recitation of Scripture. Through it, we create drama by blending words
and sentences together in much the same way as an orchestra blends
instruments. Before assigning parts, it is also helpful to explain difficult
words and work on their pronunciation. Three soloists, two choruses, and
all are needed as follows:

All: We are not among those who shrink back and so are lost, but
among those who have faith and so are saved.

Solo 1: Now faith is the assurance of things hoped for, the conviction of things not seen. Indeed, by faith our ancestors received approval.

All: By faith we understand that the worlds were prepared by the word of God, so that what is seen was made from things that are not visible.

Chorus 1: By faith Abel offered to God a more acceptable sacrifice than Cain's. Through this he received approval as righteous, God himself giving approval to his gifts; he died, but through his faith he still speaks.

Chorus 2: By faith Enoch was taken so that he did not experience death; and "he was not found, because God had taken him." For it was attested before he was taken away that "he had pleased God."

Solo 2: And without faith it is impossible to please God, for whoever would approach him must believe that he exists and that he rewards those who seek him.

Chorus 1: By faith Noah, warned by God about events as yet unseen, respected the warning and built an ark to save his household; by this he condemned the world and became an heir to the righteousness that is in accordance with faith.

Chorus 2: By faith Abraham obeyed when he was called to set out for a place that he was to receive as an inheritance; and he set out, not knowing where he was going. By faith he stayed for a time in the land he had been promised, as in a foreign land, living in tents, as did Isaac and Jacob, who were heirs with him of the same promise. For he looked forward to the city that has foundations, whose architect and builder is God.

Chorus 1: By faith he received power of procreation, even though he was too old—and Sarah herself was barren—because he considered him faithful who had promised. Therefore from one person, and this one as good as dead, descendants were born, "as many as the stars of heaven and as the innumerable grains of sand by the seashore."

Solo 3: All of these died in faith without having received the promises, but from a distance they saw and greeted them.

Solo 1: They confessed that they were strangers and foreigners on the earth, for people who speak in this way make it clear that they are seeking a homeland.

Solo 2: If they had been thinking of the land that they had left behind, they would have had opportunity to return. But as it is, they desire a better country, that is, a heavenly one.

All soloists: Therefore God is not ashamed to be called their God; indeed, he has prepared a city for them.

Chorus 1: By faith Abraham, when put to the test, offered up Isaac. He who had received the promises was ready to offer up his only son, of whom he had been told,

Solo 3: "It is through Isaac that descendants shall be named for you."

Chorus 1: He considered the fact that God is able even to raise someone from the dead—and figuratively speaking, he did receive him back.

Chorus 2: By faith Isaac invoked blessings for the future on Jacob and Esau.

Chorus 1: By faith Jacob, when dying, blessed each of the sons of Joseph, "bowing in worship over the top of his staff."

Chorus 2: By faith Joseph, at the end of his life, made mention of the exodus of the Israelites and gave instructions about his burial.

Solo 1: By faith Moses was hidden by his parents for three months after his birth, because they saw that the child was beautiful; and they were not afraid of the king's edict.

Solo 2: By faith Moses, when he was grown up, refused to be called a son of Pharaoh's daughter, choosing rather to share ill-treatment with the people of God than to enjoy the fleeting pleasures of sin.

Solo 3: He considered abuse suffered for the Christ to be greater wealth than the treasures of Egypt, for he was looking ahead to the reward.

Solo 1: By faith he left Egypt, unafraid of the king's anger; for he persevered as though he saw him who is invisible.

Solo 2: By faith he kept the Passover and the sprinkling of blood, so that the destroyer of the firstborn would not touch the firstborn of Israel.

Chorus 1: By faith the people passed through the Red Sea as if it were dry land, but when the Egyptians attempted to do so they were drowned.

Chorus 2: By faith the walls of Jericho fell after they had been encircled for seven days.

Chorus 1: By faith Rahab the prostitute did not perish with those who were disobedient, because she had received the spies in peace.

Solo 3: And what more should I say? For time would fail me to tell of Gideon, Barak, Samson, Jephthah, of David and Samuel and the prophets—who through faith conquered kingdoms, administered justice, obtained promises, shut the mouths of lions, quenched raging fire, escaped the edge of the sword, won strength out of weakness, became mighty in war, put foreign armies to flight.

Solo 1: Women received their dead by resurrection. Others were tortured, refusing to accept release, in order to obtain a better resurrection.

Solo 2: Others suffered mocking and flogging, and even chains and imprisonment. They were stoned to death, they were sawn in two, they were killed by the sword; they went about in skins of sheep and goats, destitute, persecuted, tormented—of whom the world was not worthy. They wandered in deserts and mountains, and in caves and holes in the ground.

Chorus 1: Yet all these, though they were commended for their faith, did not receive what was promised, since God had provided something better so that they would not, apart from us, be made perfect.

All: Therefore, since we are surrounded by so great a cloud of witnesses, let us also lay aside every weight and the sin that clings so closely, and let us run with perseverance the race that is set before us, looking to Jesus the pioneer and perfecter of our faith, who for the sake of the joy that was set before him endured the cross, disregarding its shame, and has taken his seat at the right hand of the throne of God.

Activity 2—Focus on the Bible Story as Mirror

In activity 2 we approach the passage from Hebrews as a mirror for looking at life meanings in Mary's, Ken's, and our own stories. Because of our participation in families and in the church, and the importance of the family's and church's roles in our lives and meaning-making, we will also look at our family's and church's story plot and meaning-making. To enter this activity, I present again the questions raised prior to the choral reading. Participants are then invited to share responses to the questions either in the whole group setting or in small groups.

Reflection Exercise

Reflect on the Scripture and consider your responses to the questions raised in the preceding section. Some responses of actual participants are as follows:

"The main theme or plot is faith in spite of all the stuff the people in the story faced. People on the Honor Roll of Faith knew that you can't get positive meaning out of life if you don't believe in something larger than life and bigger than yourself. They knew who that was—God. Granted, it's hard to keep the faith sometimes, but you can see others did it. *Faith* is a *big word* in the plot. It's like in the song we sing: 'God didn't bring me this far to leave me.'"[2]

"Another *big word* that defined the plot is *obedience* to God. The people on the Honor Roll of Faith knew that you can't get positive meaning out of life if you're not willing to live like God wants you to live. They didn't just live for themselves. They lived and did what they did with others in mind. They heard what God wanted for their lives, and they responded. They were in vocation. It's like they knew the gospel song 'I'm Gonna Live the Life God Wants Me to Live.'"

"*Perseverance* is also a *big word* in the plot. The people on the Honor Roll of Faith knew that you can't get positive meaning out of life unless you 'keep on keeping on' in life's journey in spite of all the negatives in life. It's like they were living out the spirituals 'Hold on Just a Little Bit Longer, Everything's Gonna Be All Right,' and 'Keep Hold of God's Unchanging Hand.'"

"The *big words* for me are 'God is able.' Knowing that is true is at the center of faith and hope."

Activity 3—Enter as Partner with Bible Story Actors

I invite participants to sing songs that they connected to the Scripture, or I select a revered song like those mentioned above. I then invite them to choose one of the persons on the "Honor Roll of Faith" with whom they identify. Those choosing the same person on the "Honor Roll" form a group. Each participant or group receives a prewritten depiction of the person chosen by them. They preview the depiction and determine one or more ways it reflects their own story plot and struggle for life meaning. After this, participants share the depictions and their responses with the whole group. To illustrate, six first-person depictions are provided below.[3]

Noah: I am Noah, the son of Lamech, the grandson of Methuselah, and the ninth descendant from Adam. At one point in my life, God directed me to do what seemed to be the possible. I was to prepare for a devastating flood by building an ark and taking along male and female pairs of every terrestrial and flying species. The task was *big!* But I felt sure I could do it by trusting God. I raced against time, but I finished it. Then the rains came. We were saved in that rockin' and reelin' ark.

Abraham: I am Abraham. God blessed me with many descendants. I believe God looked upon me as a friend. How could I not follow

God's divine instructions and go where God directed? So I left my home in Ur and set out on a sojourn following God's way. I didn't know where this journey was going to take me or what I was going to run into. But I discovered that it is possible to continue on because of God's guidance.

Sarah: I am Sarah, the wife of Abraham. I shared Abraham's sojourn following God. Miraculously, at ninety years of age I bore our son, Isaac. At first, I laughed that such a thing could happen. At that point in my life, I learned that the unexpected and miraculous is possible.

Jacob: I am Jacob, the son of Isaac and Rebekah. I became the father of Dinah and twelve sons whose names are those of the tribes of Israel. I admit that I have flaws. In fact, I have been called a trickster. But I am also known for being a settler-farmer, reverent worshiper of God, a hero, penitent brother, and benevolent father. One time, God gave me a dream of a ladder that showed the way from earth to heaven. I've learned something important about God in my life. Even with my flaws, God does not desert me. My life has always had promise with God.

Joseph: My name is Joseph, the oldest son of Rachel and son of Jacob. In my family, I became known as the spoiled son. This view of me became worse because Father gave me a coat of many colors and freed me from the work required of my younger brothers. I also made the situation worse by telling them about dreams showing the important turn my life was going to take. My brothers plotted to kill me, but they did not. Instead, they did something just as bad: They sold me. In spite of this, I survived and rose from a servant in a private household to a position of administrator over grain reserves in Pharaoh's court in Egypt during a time of famine. My brothers came to buy grain for their families, but they did not recognize me. They got the grain. I finally told them who I was, and we became reconciled. All during the period of family brokenness, we had each gone on with our lives. But all the while, God was working to bring us back together.

Moses: My name is Moses. I was born to a Levite couple. At first, I was hidden. But then I was set adrift on a river in a watertight container so I would not be killed in accordance with the governmental decree to kill all newborn Hebrew boys. I was picked up by Pharaoh's daughter, but I was tended by a nurse she hired. Although Pharaoh's daughter did not know it, the nurse was actually my natural mother. I was finally adopted by Pharaoh's daughter, who gave me the name of Moses.

Even though I was reared in Pharaoh's house, I found myself identifying with the enslaved people of Israel who were my brothers and sisters. In fact, because I took a drastic stand in protection of one of them, I was forced to leave Egypt. I came upon a burning bush, and I was called by God to a mission to lead the enslaved people of Israel out of Egypt to the promised land. I had to convince myself and persuade them that I was called to do this. The fact was that I had a speech impediment. God gave me the responsibility of giving them information about the journey, encouragement, chastisement when necessary, and instructions on how to get food. With God's help, we crossed the parted waters of the Red Sea out of Egypt. The people were freed from bondage.

But, even in freedom, we encountered the wilderness. Yes, we met with conflicts from outside; and there were complaints, grumblings, and rebellion from within. And yes, there were times when I got discouraged. But then seventy others came forth to share the burden of leadership. At that point, we were all in our life struggle together, leaning on God, who I know leads us and does not forsake us. I learned that our job is simply to hang in there and be faithful.

Reflection Exercise

Select one of the above first-person depictions and consider one or more ways in which the depiction reminds you of your own story plot and struggle for life meaning.

Activity 4—Envision God's Action Today

In activity 4, participants are invited to form groups of three. In the groups, they focus on the action of God in their meaning-making. They consider how their awareness of or reliance on God's acting in their lives has made possible their forming a liberating sense of meaning and purpose. In their recall, I encourage persons to tell what happened, when it happened, how they knew God was acting, how it made them feel, and in what way(s) it brought them meaning and purpose. Where further assistance is needed, wisdom is drawn from how God acted in the passage from Hebrews. That is, participants are asked to recall an instance when they experienced one or more of the following:

- Awareness of receiving God's approval (Hebrews 11:2, 4)
- Being prepared by God's Word (Hebrews 11:5), and being rewarded by God (Hebrews 11:8)
- Being warned by God about the future (Hebrews 11:8)
- Being called by God (Hebrews 11:8)
- Being empowered by God (Hebrews 11:11)
- Knowing that all cannot be counted on in this world, and that there is an everlasting city (Hebrews 11:16)
- Experiencing God's "raising you up" in the "dead" times of life (Hebrews 11:19)
- Recognition of abuse suffered by Christ (Hebrews 11:26)
- Remembering the many witnesses who have gone before (Hebrews 12:1)
- Reliance on Jesus, the pioneer and perfecter of our faith (Hebrews 12:2)

Reflection Exercise

Using the format above, consider how God has acted in your life to bring a liberating sense of meaning and purpose.

Activity 5—Anticipate Ongoing Response to God

Invite participants to consider elements in their lives that threaten positive meaning-making and purpose. To assist this endeavor, I invite them to do two things. First, they write on paper one thing that needs to be changed in their individual and community lives in order to bring positive meaning and purpose to them and others. Second, they write a prayer to God asking God to direct them, their family, and their church in addressing it.

Phase Three: Engage Christian Faith Stories from the African American Heritage

In this phase, participants link with an "African American Honor Roll of Faith." They focus on well-known and admired persons in the African American Christian faith heritage who maintained faith throughout times of trial and tribulation. They also discover the liberation mind-set and vocation strategy that motivated these persons and gave hope to persevere.

Activity 1—Disclose the Faith Heritage Story

Invite participants to link with the "African American Honor Roll of Faith" by taking part in the following litany:

Female Leader: Sojourner Truth (1797–1883) was one of millions of enslaved people who worked to birth a nation that did not honor her humanness. She spoke of her nothingness and the insignificance of her life in the eyes of those with whom she contended for the right due her and a whole people. In response, she became a vocal abolitionist, woman's rights activist, lecturer, and religious leader. She was propelled forward in freedom's struggle, woman suffrage, and ministry with unemployed and impoverished freed people by placing her perfect trust in the soul-protecting fortress of God, the Rock. This Rock raised her above the "smallness" to which the slave system sought to reduce her. Through trust in God, she found herself raised above the battlements of fear and propelled into action.

Group: Through faith, a way was made out of no way. God was the Way-Maker, and Sojourner Truth followed the Way-Maker.

Male Leader: Beaten and made to drink the bitterest dregs of slavery, Frederick Douglass (1818–1895) poured out his soul's complaint to the Almighty: "O why was I born a man, of whom to make a brute! . . . I am left in the hottest hell of unending slavery. O God, save me! God, deliver me! Let me be free! Is there any God? Why am I a slave? I will run away. I will not stand it. Get caught, or get clear,

99

I'll try it. . . . I have only one life to lose. I had as well be killed running as die standing. Only think of it; one hundred miles straight north, and I'm free. Try it? Yes! God helping me, I will. . . . There is a better day coming."[4] The time came when his hope overflowed, when all cowardice departed, and bold defiance took hold. Though still a slave, Frederick Douglass resolved that though he might remain a slave in form, the day had passed when he could be a slave in fact. He called his arrival at this point "a glorious resurrection."[5] He remained firm, and on September 3, 1838, he left his chains.[6]

Group: Through faith, a way was made out of no way. God was the Way-Maker, and Frederick Douglass followed the Way-Maker.

Female Leader: Harriet Tubman crossed the line for which she had so long dreamed. After years of cruel treatment, she was free. But she kept saying that her heart was still "down in the old cabin quarters with the old folks and my brothers and sisters."[7] Motivated by her hunger for justice, she resolved to go back to the South. She prayed to God to help her, saying, "Oh, dear Lord, I ain't got no friend but you. Come to my help, Lord, for I'm in trouble!"[8] Between 1850 and 1860, she was a daring conductor on the Underground Railroad, through which she guided more than three hundred slaves, including her parents, to freedom. There was a reward of twelve thousand dollars offered for her in Maryland. It was said that she would probably be burned alive if caught. But this heroine, whom the slaves called Moses, was not deterred from her call to act. And she was never caught.[9] Once a trip was started, there was no turning back. And if someone got cold feet, the voice of "Moses" rang in their ears, "Move or die!"[10] She sang to bolster the spirits of her followers, and they joined in the spiritual "Go Down Moses": "You may hinder me here, but you can't up there, Let my people go. He sits in the heavens and answers prayer. Let my people go! Oh, go down, Moses. Way down in Egypt land. Tell old Pharaoh, 'Let my people go!'"

Group: Through faith, a way was made out of no way. God was the Way-Maker, and Harriet Tubman followed the Way-Maker.

Male Leader: And what more should we say? If there were time, we would tell of Dr. James W. C. Pennington, fugitive slave, teacher, clergyman, author, and civil rights activist; James Weldon Johnson, poet and composer; Mary McLeod Bethune, educator, civil and woman's rights activist, government official, and school founder; Booker T. Washington, proponent of self-improvement and racial solidarity; and W. E. B. DuBois, scholar and activist.

Female Leader: We would tell of George Washington Carver, botanist; Zora Neal Hurston, author; Ralph Bunche, statesman and United Nations ambassador; Adam Clayton Powell Jr., political leader and minister; Fannie Lou Hamer, civil rights activist, sharecropper; Lorraine Hansberry, playwright, activist; Jesse Owens, Olympic gold medalist; Rosa Parks, civil rights activist and advocate for justice; Martin Luther King Jr., minister and civil rights leader; Thurgood Marshall, lawyer and United States Supreme Court Justice; and countless more whom we name in our hearts.

Both Leaders: These are they who, through faith, continued to build up a bowed-down people, followed a vision of God's promise while enduring human hostility, refused to relinquish the struggle for justice in an unjust society, and won strength out of weakness even in the face of recrimination and death.

All: Through faith, a way was made out of no way for this cloud of witnesses. God was the Way-Maker, and they followed the Way-Maker. Our future lies before us. Will we, like those before us, persevere, looking to Jesus, the pioneer and perfecter of our faith?

Activity 2—Describe the Liberation Mind-Set

In activity 2, three key questions are posed:

1. What is the liberation mind-set that all on the "African American Honor Roll of Faith" had in common?

2. How did this mind-set inform their life meanings and purposes?
3. What are some futile mind-sets and negative life meanings and purposes the Honor Roll challenges today?

Actual participants have responded as follows:

"All on the Honor Roll had a liberation mind-set focused on freeing brothers and sisters from shackles that precluded human dignity. They wanted to assure an opportunity for brothers and sisters to participate in life unhindered by racism and the lack of life's basic necessities. This mind-set gave direction to their story plot. Meaning in their lives was derived from their own vision of liberation and their carrying out of that vision."

"The Honor Roll challenges each one of us and our churches to break out of mind-sets of self-centeredness, reluctance, and fear of acting on behalf of others. These mind-sets lead to futility because when one of us is hurting, all hurt."

"The liberation mind-set is a family thing, too. Harriet Tubman's close relatives and people outside it became extended family for whom she felt keen responsibility."

"Deep-lasting meaning comes when we know we are helping one another. The Honor Roll convicts us to do more."

Activity 3—Describe the Liberation Mind-Set and Vocational Strategies That Bring Hope and Liberation

Ask the participants to share their responses to the following:

- What generating theme made it possible for those on the "African-American Honor Roll of Faith" to act on their mind-set?
- How does this theme and their acting on it challenge us today?

Reflection Exercise

How would you answer the questions posed above? Actual participants have stated the following:

"As in the Hebrews passage, faith in God, obedience to God, and perseverance were generating themes in the lives of those on the 'African-American Honor Roll of Faith.' This theme allowed them to 'keep on keeping on' in spite of difficult obstacles and hardship."

"Their strategy was one of really seeing the need for action and acknowledging their responsibility to act. They did not cave in, and because they kept their eye on 'God, the Rock,' as Sojourner Truth put it, they had a sense of power, resolve, and direction."

"Both the Scripture 'Honor Roll of Faith' and the 'African American Honor Roll of Faith' give us a tremendous challenge as individuals and congregations to do likewise."

"What about family members? I think we need to have a new understanding of family and take to heart our responsibility to act for the future of close-up family members and others who really are our extended family. If we are to have hope for the future and are serious about liberation, then we must be serious about family."

Phase Four: Engage in Christian Ethical Decision Making

In this final phase of the story-linking process, we focus on making decisions aimed toward positive meaning-making and life purpose based on a liberating story plot. We give particular attention to what God is calling us to do in this regard and to concrete actions we need to take.

Activity 1—Discern God's Call

Invite participants to call to memory as much as they can about the Scripture passage from Hebrews and the "African American Honor Roll of Faith." After the period of silent memory summation, ask each participant to choose a partner. Ask the partners to share with each other two or three points in the Scripture and the "African-American Honor Roll of Faith" that particularly challenged them to look at their story plot. Partners also may be asked to respond to the questions:

• What in the Scripture inspires you to act differently?

- Who would you want to emulate in the "African American Honor Roll of Faith"? Why?

Activity 2—Decide on Concrete Actions

Participants decide ways of responding to God's call to attend to their story plot or to change it. Participants refer to their written responses from activity 5 in phase two. At that time, they are asked to write one thing needing change in their individual, family, congregational, and community lives in order to bring positive meaning and purpose to them and others. In this activity, further response is given on paper or with a partner according to the following:

- Identify two concrete actions you can take and two concrete actions family members, your congregation, and/or community residents can take to effect change in the matter you identified.
- Decide how far you will go to carry out the actions and how you can engage family members, your congregation, and/or community residents in action.
- Examine how the actions will contribute to a future of hope and liberation for you and others.
- Determine why these actions are important from a Christian viewpoint or what meanings you assign to them.

The story-linking process concludes with voluntary participant sharing and songs such as "Order My Steps,"[11] and "I Will Trust in the Lord 'Til I Die."[12]

Follow-Up Suggestions

In an intergenerational group, ask participants to form small groups and explore and list meanings assigned to life from the perspective of African American children, teens, young adults, middle adults, and older adults. Substitute the scripture Isaiah 40:27-31. Jeremiah 8:22; 29:11-13; and Philippians 3:13b-14 may also be used. These scriptures have particular meaning because they address the central meaning-making theme of having wisdom in the form of spiritual resources to continue on in the midst of hardship. Because of their perseverance and spiritual resource themes, the spirituals "Walk Together Children"[13] and "There Is a Balm in Gilead,"[14] or the African American heritage poem "Mother to Son (or Daughter)" by Langston Hughes[15] may be used for the heritage story.

CHAPTER 5

THE PIVOTAL ROLE OF SCRIPTURE IN STORY-LINKING AND HOW TO CHOOSE SCRIPTURE

When knowledge comes, the whole world is turned upside down. The meaning of things begins to emerge. And more importantly, the relations between things are seen for the first time.

—Howard Thurman
The Inward Journey

In story-linking, the Bible is a pivotal sense-making document. It reveals the Story of God through Jesus Christ. We enter it with our stories and case studies to discover wisdom to guide us on the journey of life. The Bible assists our recognition of insights from African American Christian faith heritage stories. From our linking with the Bible, we are challenged to see its impact on our lives and discern how to embody its message in our lives.

We link with the Bible by bringing our everyday stories as African Americans with us. We enter the Bible with our joys. We also enter with our struggles related to experiences of oppression in this country and other everyday life struggles that block and bind us. We view and respond to the Bible through the lens of all that makes up our identities, social contexts, interpersonal relationships, life events, life meanings, and story plots.

The Bible has historically held special importance for the approach of African Americans to freedom from oppression and struggles. During slavery, African Americans found in the Bible a liberation pathway. Linking with the Bible became an important and dynamic way through which they heard God's call to liberation, imagined God directing and sustaining them, and decided their vocational response to God. Contemporary story-linking is a way of opening to us these same kinds of experiences with the Bible.

But what Bible stories and texts should we choose? On what basis do we choose? There are numerous stories/texts in the Bible that can place us in touch with God's speaking to us. There are also numerous accounts of biblical sojourners whose stories tell of oppressive existence, life struggles, and their quest for liberation and vocation. In this chapter, we will look at three approaches to choosing Scripture for use in story-linking processes. These approaches include a historical-cultural approach, a lectionary approach, and a uniform lesson materials approach. Throughout, attention will be given to the questions: How may leaders/teachers prepare for using Scripture in story-linking? What part may leaders/teachers prepare for using Scripture in story-linking? What part may leaders/teachers and participants play in selecting Scripture?

A Historical-Cultural Approach to Choosing Scripture

One way of determining what Bible stories/texts to use for story-linking in African American settings is to look for stories/texts already chosen by African Americans across the years. This is best accomplished by looking at African American cultural expressions such as spirituals, hymns, gospel songs, sermons, poems, and folk sayings for references to Scripture within them.

Dating back to slavery, African Americans have had a strong biblical orientation and have relied on specific stories/texts for help in the throes of trials and tribulations. A variety of cultural expressions of African Americans show how they linked with specific Bible stories/texts. Their choices of Scripture were cultural choices. When we select Bible stories/texts for contemporary story-linking processes from the wealth of cultural choices, we are making *historical-cultural choices* of Scripture. There are at least five categories of choices:

1. Old Testament freedom stories;
2. Old Testament and New Testament counter-freedom stories;
3. Old Testament declaration stories;
4. The New Testament salvation story; and
5. New Testament Christian lifestyle stories

In this chapter, we will become aware of some choices of Scripture made by African Americans from slavery onward using these categories. We will also note cultural expressions that relate to the scriptural material and that are useful in story-linking. Some of the scriptural material identified herein was incorporated in story-linking processes in chapters 2 through 4 and some were suggested for follow-up processes. Notations will be made about this use.

In preparing to use Bible stories or texts presented in this chapter, leaders/teachers will find probing the texts helpful for finding answers to the following questions:

- How does the Bible story/text address African American identity, social contexts, interpersonal relationships, life events, life meanings, and story plots?
- What wisdom does the Bible story/text provide for dealing with issues arising in these facets of everyday stories?
- What hints does the story/text give about what liberation means and how it is attained in the various facets of life?
- What hints does the story/text give about what vocation means and how it is enacted in ways that build hope in the various facets of life?
- What relationships can be drawn between liberating wisdom, liberation, and hope-building vocation in the story/text?

When we engage in this kind of preparatory study, we may find that certain stories/texts address a particular dimension of life, while others address more than one dimension. Suggestions for life examples are made with each scripture indicated on the charts below.

Once a Bible story/text and the life dimension with which to link it are chosen, it should be incorporated into the story-linking process as illustrated in the preceding chapters. Songs, sermon material, poems, and cultural sayings may be incorporated along with Bible stories and texts, or they may be used in conjunction with African American Christian faith heritage stories.

Old Testament Freedom Stories

Old Testament freedom stories are stories that disclose symbols of liberation used by African Americans. Liberating wisdom is found in their depiction of the nature of hope-building vocation through focus on leadership, relationship with God, and traits needed in the struggle to overcome oppression and adversity. Chart 1 gives examples of Old Testament freedom stories/texts and cultural expressions reflecting them.

CHART 1
OLD TESTAMENT FREEDOM STORIES

Old Testament Freedom Stories	Cultural Expressions
Moses' call and the freedom struggle of the Israelites, as told in Exodus 3:1-12; 13:17-22; 14:1-31	Spiritual—"Go Down, Moses"[1]
Journey out of the wilderness into the promised land by God's commission of Joshua, as told in Joshua 1 through 4 (Use in story-linking focused on interpersonal relations, life events, life meanings, and story plots.)	Sermons—"The God Who Takes Off Chariot Wheels" by D. E. King,[2] and "That Was Then, This Is Now" by Lance Watson[3]
Daniel in the lions' den, as told in chapter 6 of the book of Daniel (Use with identity, social contexts, interpersonal relations and life events.)	Spiritual—"Didn't My Lord Deliver Daniel?"[4]
David and Goliath, as told in 1 Samuel 17:1-51 (Use with interpersonal relations, life events, life meanings, and story plots.)	Spiritual—"Little David, Play on Your Harp"[5] Sermon—"Giants Keep Coming" by William Watley[6]
The three Hebrew boys (Shadrach, Meshach, and Abednego) in the	Incorporated into the prior cited spiritual—"Didn't My Lord

fiery furnace, as told in Daniel 3:1-30 (Use with identity, social contexts, interpersonal relations, and life events)	Deliver Daniel?" Sermon—"Faith Under Fire" by Jeremiah A. Wright[7]
Jonah in and out of the belly of the whale, as found in the four short chapters 1 through 4 in the book of Jonah (Use with every facet of the everyday stories.)	Incorporated into the prior cited spiritual—"Didn't My Lord Deliver Daniel?"

Old Testament and New Testament Counter-Freedom Stories

African American Christians across the years have also chosen counter-freedom stories in Scripture. The gist of these stories appears in African American preaching material and oral folk sayings. The stories are characterized by bondage and subservience themes by which persons in the larger social structure have justified oppression. Meanings are assigned to these stories/texts in light of counter-liberation themes marking the everyday stories of African Americans. These meanings invariably depict an understanding of the positive value God places on us over against devaluation by other humans. In short, the counter-freedom stories are typical of biblical texts with which we have historically critically engaged for inside our experiences. In the engagement process, we deviate from literal interpretations, thereby giving new light to texts that contradict our understanding of God's value and liberating activity through Jesus for *all*. The following are examples of counter-freedom stories:

- "Curse of Ham" found in Genesis 9:20-27;
- Paul's encouragement of slaves to be obedient to their masters, found in Ephesians 6:5 and Colossians 3:22; and
- Paul's sending the slave Onesimus back to his master, detailed in the book of Philemon.

One example of an African American folk saying focuses on reinterpreting the counter-liberation story of Hagar and Ishmael, found in Genesis 16:1-6 and 21:8-21. The folk saying was handed down to me through my maternal grandmother and was one shared by other African Americans in the Indiana town of my birth. In the folk saying, Hagar was given the affectionate name of "Aunt Haggie" and Ishmael was referred to as "Aunt Haggie's child," and therefore one with whom we are related. Entitled "Aunt Haggie," the folk saying is as follows:

> People may treat you like they did "Aunt Haggie" or like one of "Aunt Haggie's children," but you don't have to act like you're not important or be ashamed of who you are, you hear? You just remember, you're one of God's children.

Like the liberation stories in the Bible, the counter-freedom stories may be chosen for use in contemporary story-linking processes. They are an important way of opening to persons a way of talking about dehumanizing and hurtful attitudes and treatment and what the wisdom of the Bible is for their response to these attitudes and treatment. Recall that both the text from Genesis and the African American folk saying are suggested as follow-up material at the end of chapter 2, which focuses on identity and social contexts.

Old Testament Declaration Stories

Historical-cultural choices of biblical material also include texts that declare feelings, attitudes, desires, and behaviors often associated with the struggle for liberation and vocation. Some of the texts declare often inexplicable agony and hurt amid trial and tribulation. This type of declaration story has a theme of theodicy, which means suffering and anguish. Other declaration stories reveal the possibility and, indeed, the presence of guidance, assurance, thanksgiving, and jubilation in life's sojourn. This second type of declaration story exemplifies themes of promise and celebration. Texts from the Psalms and Jeremiah have been among the most popular choices of declaration stories. African American choices of texts with theodicy themes show that faith does not always cancel disappointment, oppression, and bondage, and that we do not always see concretely God's liberating work. In story-linking, these stories offer an avenue for persons to give voice openly to their laments to God at times when their faith in God's righteousness is not easy and they are in search of wisdom. Examples of declaration stories with theodicy themes and related cultural expressions appear in chart 2.

CHART 2
OLD TESTAMENT DECLARATION STORIES/TEXTS
WITH THEODICY THEMES

Old Testament Declaration Stories with Theodicy Themes	*Cultural Expressions*
Psalm 22:1-11 (Use with all facets of the everyday stories.)	Spiritual—"Sometimes I Feel Like Motherless Child"[8]
Psalm 13 (Use with all facets of the everyday stories.)	Slave narratives—"Oh, Lord, how long?"[9] and "Oh, Lord Jesus, how long, how long, how long shall I suffer this way?"[10] Songs—"Come By Here (Kum bah-ya)"[11] and "Grant Me a Blessing"[12]
Jeremiah 8:22 (Use with all facets of the everyday stories.)	Black slaves answered the question posed in the Scripture as they sang the spiritual "There is a balm in Gilead to make the wounded whole, There is a balm in Gilead to heal the sinsick soul. Sometimes I feel discouraged and think my works in vain. But then the Holy Spirit revives my soul again."[13]

Recall that Psalm 13 is suggested for follow-up at the end of chapter 3, which focuses on interpersonal relationships and life events. In chapter 4 on life meanings and story plots, Jeremiah 8:22 is suggested as a follow-up companion text with a New Testament text and along with the spiritual "Balm in Gilead" and sermon material. However, any of the texts mentioned above may be considered for follow-up in chapters 2 through 4.

African Americans choose texts in which promise and celebration are found. Of particular significance are texts in the books of Psalms and Isaiah. These texts have historically provided a "bowed-down" people resources to "keep on keeping on" in the midst of trial and tribulation. In story-linking, the texts appropriately function as companions to counter-freedom stories and declaration stories with theodicy themes.

African American choices of declaration stories that have promise and celebration themes are reflected particularly in spirituals, gospel songs, and sermon material. For this reason, singing spirituals and gospel songs and looking at sermon materials are important additions to the process of linking with these scriptures. Chart 3 below contains examples of texts that may be considered declaration stories with themes of promise or celebration. Cultural expressions reflecting the themes accompany the Bible texts as does one sermon title.

CHART 3
OLD TESTAMENT DECLARATION STORIES WITH THEMES OF PROMISE OR CELEBRATION

Old Testament Declaration Stories with Themes of Promise or Celebration	*Cultural Expressions*
Psalm 23 (Use with all facets of the everyday stories.)	Song—"We Shall Walk Through the Valley in Peace"[14] Sermon—"The Lord Is My Shepherd" by Clay Evans[15]
Psalm 27 (Use with all facets of the everyday stories.)	Song—"I Will Trust in the Lord"[16] Also, the gospel song—"The Lord Is My Light"[17]
Psalms 33 and 104 (See suggestion for Psalm 33:13-22 as follow-up at end of chapter 3.)	Spiritual—"He's Got the Whole World in His Hands"[18]
Isaiah 40:27-31 (See suggestions for use of text	Spiritual—"Walk Together Children"[19]

and song at end of chapter 4.)
Jeremiah 29:11
(Use with life meanings and
story plot.)

Sermon—"God Calls Us to Be
Eagles" by William Watley[20]
Song—"Hold to God's Unchanging
Hand"[21]
Sermon—"The Power of Purpose"
by Linda Gobodo[22]

The New Testament Salvation Story

For African Americans, the New Testament salvation story emphasizes
the person of Jesus. This includes Jesus' parables, sayings, acts, and character that herald him as the great champion of freedom. Underlying the
salvation story is the historical understanding among African Americans
that Jesus as champion of freedom shows us how to live liberating stories
and hope-building vocations. Options of Bible texts that show this understanding, along with cultural expressions reflecting it, are contained in
charts 4A, 4B, and 4C below.

CHART 4A
NEW TESTAMENT SALVATION STORY: PARABLES
AND SAYINGS OF JESUS

Parables and Sayings of Jesus	*Cultural Expressions*
Matthew 7:24-27 or Luke 6:46-49 (Use with every facet of the everyday story.)	Songs: "I Got a Home in-a Dat Rock Don't You See"[23] and "Jesus Is a Rock in a Weary Land"[24]
Matthew 5:14-16 (See suggestions for use in chapter 2.)	Spiritual: "This Little Light of Mine"[25]
Matthew 22:1-14 or Luke 14:15-24 (Use with story-linking focused on identity and social context.)	Spiritual: "I'm A-Going to Eat at the Welcome Table"[26]

CHART 4B
NEW TESTAMENT SALVATION STORY: ACTS OF JESUS

Acts of Jesus

Cultural Expressions

Mark 4:35-41;
Matthew 9:2-8; or
Luke 5:17-26
(Use with story-linking
focused on identity and social
contexts, interpersonal
relationships, and life events.)

Gospel hymns: "When the Storms
of Life Are Raging, Stand by Me,"[27]
and "'Tis the Ol' Ship of Zion"
(see especially verse 2),[28]
and "Peace! Be Still"[29]

Mark 2:1-12;
Matthew 9:2-8; or Luke 8:22-25
(See suggestion for use in
chapter 3.)

Gospel song: "We Won't Leave
Here Like We Came"[30]

CHART 4C
NEW TESTAMENT SALVATION STORY:
THE CHARACTER OF JESUS

Character of Jesus

Cultural Expressions

John 1:1-5,
Jesus as Light
(Use with all facets of
everyday stories.)

Gospel song: "Walk in the Light,
Beautiful Light"[31]

Luke 12:4-7 and
Matthew 10:26-31,
Jesus as Friend
(Use with all facets of
everyday stories.)

Gospel song, "His Eye Is on the
Sparrow"[32]

Matthew 25:1-13, Jesus, the
Challenger of persons to tend to
vocation
(Use with all facets of
everyday stories.)

Spiritual: "Members, Don't Get
Weary 'Til Your Work Is Done"[33]

Luke 18:35-43; Matthew 20:29-34; or Mark 10:46-52. See also: Luke 17:11-16 and Mark 2:1-12, Jesus as powerful, caring, and merciful (See suggested use of Mark 2:1-12 in chapter 3.)	Traditional African American song: "I'm So Glad, Jesus Lifted Me,"[34] and gospel song: "He Looked Beyond My Fault and Saw My Need"[35]
Luke 2:8-20. Also Mark 15:16-39; Matthew 27:27-56; Luke 23:26-49; or John 19:16b-30: Jesus as vulnerable, humble, and sacrificial (Use with every facet of the everyday story.)	Gospel songs: "The Lamb,"[36] "Just For Me,"[37] and the spiritual: "He Never Said a Mumbalin' Word"[38]
Mark 14:22-26; Matthew 26:26-29; or Luke 22:14-23: Jesus as com- memorator of God's liberating love (Use with every facet of the everyday story.)	Spiritual: "Let Us Break Bread Together"[39]
Luke 23:26-34: Jesus as forgiving Savior (Use with every facet of the everyday story.)	Hymn: "Amazing Grace";[40] Gospel song: "Your Grace and Mercy";[41] and traditional song: "Remember Me"[42]

New Testament Christian Lifestyle Stories

Historically, African Americans have chosen New Testament texts that describe the nature of the Christian life one is expected to live regardless of one's situation. The spirituals in particular show that Christian life is lived after the example of Jesus Christ, the champion of freedom. They reveal liberating wisdom, show God's plan for liberation, and emphasize that hope-building vocation is carried forward through committed Christian living by *all* who accept God's call. That includes us! Biblical texts and cultural expressions appear in chart 5 below.

CHART 5
NEW TESTAMENT CHRISTIAN LIFESTYLE STORIES

Christian Lifestyle	*Cultural Expressions*
Ephesians 4:11-16: Live in Christ's fullness (Use with every facet of the everyday story.)	The theme of the biblical text is found in a poem by former slave Walter L. Brooks titled "The Stature of the Fullness of Christ."[43] Spiritual: "Lord, I Want to Be a Christian"[44]
Galatians 6:1-10: Live by the Spirit of Jesus in community (Use with every facet of the everyday story.)	Spiritual: "Walk Together, Children";[45] gospel song: "Give Me a Clean Heart";[46] and spiritual: "Guide My Feet, While I Run This Race"[47]
Hebrews 10:39; 11:1-39; 12:1-2: Live by faith, commitment, perseverance (See suggestions for use of the text in chapter 4.)	Spiritual: "I Will Trust in the Lord";[48] and gospel songs: "We've Come This Far by Faith,"[49] and "I Don't Feel No Ways Tired"[50]

Prospects and Problems of Using the Historical-Cultural Approach to Choosing Scripture

The historical-cultural approach to choosing Bible texts is a pivotal prospect for story-linking processes. It is pivotal because it takes full account of the African American cultural context. It helps leaders/teachers and participants to correlate Scripture with the biblically oriented and culturally rich African American tradition. The approach holds potential for heightening our awareness of how African Americans, past and present, have linked with Scripture. It promotes claiming our cultural and biblical roots as African Americans.

The historical-cultural approach also opens the way for leaders/teachers *and* participants to draw on revered Bible stories and texts, biblically based songs, cultural sayings, and sermon material related to the Bible. In this way, choosing Bible stories is not the sole responsibility of leaders/teachers. Instead, leaders/teachers encourage participants to contribute materials they bring. Participants bring into the story-linking processes the biblical and cultural resources that are important to them, and they share why these resources are important. Moreover, when participants take part in story-linking in this way, the process becomes their process.

The historical-cultural approach is most easily employed in Christian education settings where leaders/teachers and participants are knowledgeable of biblical and cultural resources. That is, the approach is best carried forth when persons have had prior experiences with Bible storytelling and story-listening, African American faith heritage songs, cultural sayings, and sermons. Problems of accessing, choosing, and using appropriately these resources may arise in settings where leaders/teachers or participants have had limited exposure and involvement with them. Nonetheless, the problems can be overcome through two steps initiated by leaders/teachers.

The first step is to seek biblical and cultural materials in libraries and bookstores and carefully review the materials. Commentaries and reference works on these materials are also helpful. The purpose for reviewing the materials is to determine how biblical materials and cultural resources such as heritage songs, cultural sayings, and sermon material relate to one another. This means seeking to answer the questions: What Bible stories or texts are reflected in these cultural resources? How are the stories told in the cultural resources? Why?

The second step is to identify facets of the everyday African American stories with which the Bible texts and cultural materials may be linked. The way to do this is through seeing similarities between issues addressed in Bible texts and cultural materials and those addressed in the everyday stories. It is helpful to link the biblical and cultural materials with all facets of everyday African American stories to which they give guidance. Repetitive use of both biblical and cultural materials reminds leaders/teachers and participants that Scripture speaks to us in many different ways. Repetition also contributes to our remembering these materials and claiming them as vital instructional agents in our quests for liberating wisdom and liberation and hope-building vocation.

The Lectionary Approach to Choosing Scripture

Particularly in settings where experiences with biblical and cultural resources are limited, consulting the lectionary offers another approach to choosing Scripture for story-linking processes. The lectionary is a list of selected Bible texts for each Sunday of the church year. The Bible texts entered for each Sunday include a psalm, a text from the Old Testament, one from the New Testament Epistles, and one from the New Testament Gospels. These selections form what is called the Revised Common Lectionary. The lectionary is generally established for a three-year period, according to a triennial calendar labeled as years A, B, and C. The calendars are often found in church hymnbooks and other church worship materials. They provide a guide that shows which texts are to be used on a given Sunday.

In using the Revised Common Lectionary in story-linking, we actually link facets of everyday African American stories with biblical stories that correspond with the various seasons of the Christian year. That is, biblical material focused around the seasons of Advent, Christmas, Epiphany, Lent, Easter, Pentecost, and other special days provide the overall framework for story-linking processes. We still pose the questions: What wisdom is found in the Scripture and what does the Scripture have to say for liberation and hope-building vocation in terms of our identities, social contexts, interpersonal relations, life events, and story plots? However, the lectionary approach invites the added question: How do the various seasons of the Christian year and the church's observance of them contribute to our liberation and vocation in these facets of our lives?

Prospects and Problems of Using the Lectionary Approach to Choosing Scripture for Story-Linking

A primary contribution of the lectionary approach to story-linking processes is its provision of predetermined Bible texts. Since they are already provided in the lectionary, leaders/teachers do not have to decide on Bible texts. The lectionary approach also challenges us to incorporate Bible stories that are new to us and offer us new ways of seeing our everyday stories. And the lectionary invites us to consider whether and how our African American believing communities interpret our everyday lives, our liberation, and vocation in light of the Christian year.

A key problem in using the lectionary approach is the dominance of the Christian calendar. Because of this dominance, it may not be possible to incorporate in fullest measure historic culturally revered Bible texts and other cultural materials. Nonetheless, it is possible for leaders/teachers to employ a planning method that can maximize the use of important contextual materials in story-linking processes. This method builds on one proposed by Dieter T. Hessel and incorporates the following:

1. Experience and question the Bible story with focus on finding out what is going on in the text. Take note of the setting, story movement, and story actors.
2. Explore whether and how the story addresses identity, social contexts, interpersonal relationships, life events, life meanings, and story plot. Take note of evidences of liberating wisdom, liberating activity, and vocation.
3. Explore in commentaries the role of the story/text in its biblical setting.
4. Discover what God is doing in the story/text.
5. Discern what the text says for decisions you may make that can bring about greater and ongoing experiences of liberation and vocation.
6. Reflect critically on the church's faithful response to the Bible story/text in its life of worship, education, and nurture during the Christian season being emphasized.
7. Discern what changes are needed in the life of the church to promote liberation and vocation in the various facets of everyday life.[51]

The Uniform Lesson Series Approach to Choosing Scripture for Story-Linking

A third approach to choosing Scripture for story-linking processes entails use of Scripture contained in uniform lesson series. Like the lectionary approach, the uniform lesson series approach does not require leaders/teachers to select Bible texts. The texts are preselected in a way that is designed to cover the entire Bible in a six-year cycle. During the cycle, nearly every book of the Bible is dealt with in some fashion within church school and Bible study materials for the various age levels.

Prospects and Problems of Using the Uniform Lesson Approach in Choosing Scripture for Story-Linking

The uniform lesson approach provides a helpful alternative approach to choosing Scripture for story-linking processes because many local churches use the uniform lesson series in church school. This means that the series is already available to leaders/teachers and participants. Since the series is designated to cover the whole Bible during a six-year cycle, and incorporates planned lessons, historic culturally revered Bible stories will be included. Moreover, the series invites linking with unfamiliar texts.

The problem is, texts that have particular contextual meaning may not appear when they are desired or when they may have greatest impact. Nonetheless, the approach does not preclude leaders'/teachers' use of the seven-step planning approach described above in order to assure applicability to the precise concerns of story-linking.

Reflection Exercise

Consider the three approaches to choosing Scripture for story-linking processes. Enter into some time to plan a story-linking experience based on each one of the approaches. After you choose the scripture, be sure to experience the scripture and determine which life dimension(s) it addresses. Then, consider how you will present it in phase two of the story-linking process as outlined at the end of chapter 1. You may wish to refer again to the illustrations of the story-linking process in chapters 2 through 4.

C H A P T E R   6

MEDIATING GROUP PROCESSES

*Our shoulders touch but our hearts cry out for understanding without which
there can be no life and no meaning. . . . There must be found ever-creative
ways that can ventilate the private soul without blowing it away, that can confirm and affirm the integrity of the person.*

—Howard Thurman
The Inward Journey

In guiding groups through the story-linking process, I have found that
groups and individuals within them differ in how they engage the
process and interact with one another. Some whole groups "dive in"
with exuberant participation. Others are less talkative in the beginning and
gradually "grow into" open and in-depth participation. Some individuals
are readily self-disclosive while others are not; and some prefer quiet reflection to more expressive forms. Some individuals also enjoy and have capac-
ities for facilitating small groups while others prefer the participant role.

The groups reminded me of the importance of paying attention to
group processes and dynamics in implementing the story-linking model.
Indeed, I believe attentiveness to group processes and dynamics is essential if we are to create an environment in which liberating wisdom can be
discerned. It is important that we engage story-linking in ways that
embody the essence of liberation and make possible our grasp of the hope
in our choices and exercise of vocation. But what is meant by group
processes and group dynamics, and how do we take them into account as
leaders/teachers in the story-linking process?

The term "group processes" refers to the strategies or plan of action leaders/teachers take to ensure an emancipatory environment. The term "group dynamics" refers to the forces and conditions that influence how group members participate and relate with one another in the story-linking process. We cannot separate the two because each impacts the other. This chapter presents seven elements that I have found helpful in attending to group processes and dynamics. These elements include approaches to convening groups, knowing developmental stages of groups, tending to group membership and size, time management, constructing inviting physical settings, caring for those who struggle with their stories, and encouraging follow-up.

Approaches to Convening Groups

How we get started in the story-linking process is important. It can make a difference in persons' decisions to enter and fully engage in the process in a group setting and elsewhere. One pivotal approach to convening groups entails the leader's welcoming presence. Another key approach involves sharing the nature of the story-linking process into which persons are being invited. A final approach is to invite interpersonal connection.

The Welcoming Presence of Leaders/Teachers

The role of the leader or teacher includes offering a welcoming presence. This means that we value and appreciate those who join us in the story-linking process as they are, and we express openly our appreciation for their presence with us and for the opportunity to relate together. The welcoming presence of the leader/teacher reflects the Christian understanding of agape love mentioned in the prologue. Stated another way, the practice of agape love through a welcoming presence becomes an important promoter of liberation and vocation-centered action within the group.

Our role as a welcoming presence based on agape love also means that we are not hesitant to say and to show through our nonverbal expressions that we are glad to be together. Expressions of positive value and appreciation of persons is particularly important in African American

Christian education settings because of the negative valuing we often receive in everyday social contexts.

Positive valuing and expressions of appreciation given by leaders/teachers are a way of affirming our being in solidarity. These are also ways of saying to persons that their presence is not being taken for granted. This kind of welcoming presence encourages openness in communication among participants and builds within them a sense of security. With this presence, we recognize that persons are most guarded when they feel unsure of how they will be received.

Sharing the Nature of the Story-Linking Process

Because story-linking is a particular approach to Christian education, it is helpful to let participants know the nature of the process. This gives participants a glimpse of where we are headed in the process as well as offering them tools with which to engage in story-linking on their own. It is important for leaders/teachers to share with participants that they are invited into a four-phase story-linking process. This means that they will look at everyday African American stories. They will link these stories with the Christian faith story contained in the Bible. They will also link with African American Christian faith heritage stories. And they will learn to practice Christian decision making. Actually, it is wise to reidentify the four story-linking phases at the beginning of each session.

Participants need to know, as well, that story-linking focuses on our discernment of liberating wisdom and on liberation and vocation in the various facets of our everyday stories. For this reason, it is important that we share with groups that we will invite them into dialogue about meanings of liberating wisdom and where we find it as well as what liberation and vocation mean.

As stated earlier, story-linking is appropriately undertaken in settings where intentional efforts are made to create an environment where agape love is practiced. In such an environment, we give people voice and we commit to hear and to respond to them with care, support, and attentive listening. How do we begin to create this environment?

INVITING PERSONS INTO INTERPERSONAL CONNECTION

I like to begin each story-linking session with a short period (not exceeding ten minutes) during which group members engage in what I call "Making Interpersonal Connections." Thus, the first phase of the story-linking process begins only after the group has "connected." Making interpersonal connections can be whole-group oriented or they may be partner or small group oriented.

MAKING INTERPERSONAL CONNECTIONS IN WHOLE GROUP SETTINGS

Making interpersonal connections in groups encompasses the need for participants to disclose something about themselves before the whole group. The disclosures may begin with "connection starters" given by the leader/teacher, of which the following are examples:

- Invite group members to complete starters like:
  "I am . . ."
  "One thing you may not know about me is . . ."
  "The person I admire most is . . ." and "I admire that person because . . ."
  "The best thing about my life is . . ."
  "The most challenging thing about my life is . . ."
- Invite group members to tell about an occurrence in the previous week or recent past that gave them joy, assurance, or hope.
- Invite group members to share a concern for which they desire group prayer.
- Invite group members to tell the names and words of their favorite religious songs or Bible verses and why they are favorites. This may be followed by singing songs with which all group members are familiar.

Making interpersonal connections in the whole group helps us learn about one another, even if we are related or have been previously acquainted. It also builds group openness, fosters responsiveness toward one another, and promotes group solidarity. After each member's disclosure, group members may be invited to respond by saying, "Thank you for sharing."

MAKING INTERPERSONAL CONNECTIONS IN SMALL GROUPS

Participants may also make interpersonal connections with a partner or in a small group of no more than four persons. In this instance, leaders/

teachers guide persons to share something about themselves with a partner or small group members. The connection starters above may be used for this purpose. It is preferable to form different partners and different small group membership if you use that format repeatedly.

Partner and small group connections emphasize caring, attentive listening, and developing the ability to reflect back what another has shared. Thus partners and small group members are invited to practice repeating what they hear others say and receiving clarification from others when needed. It is also helpful to invite partners and small group members to determine ways of giving caring, affirming, and supportive responses to one another. Persons might respond to one another by saying, for example: "I appreciate what you shared," or "Thank you for sharing." They might also agree to say prayers of thanks or prayers of intercession for one another.

Reflection Exercise

Develop a specific strategy that you might use to convene a group in which you intend to use the story-linking process.

Knowing Developmental Stages of Groups

How leaders/teachers mediate group processes depends on a complex set of factors. Some of the key factors include how long a group has been together, whether the leader/teacher is new to her or his role with a group, what kind of interpersonal style has been developed in groups of long-standing, and what kind of interpersonal style the leader/teacher fosters.

It is also good to recognize that groups typically develop in stages. Newly constituted groups with whom leaders/teachers have had no prior contact typically go through an initial stage of orientation or encounter. New groups may then move to a stage characterized by conflict, dominance, and differentiation. During a third stage, group members may move to a sense of group cohesiveness and group productivity. Finally, a group may move to a stage characterized by free and constructive movement between independence and interdependence. Awareness of these stages provides bases for deciding what is needed to mediate group processes and respond to group dynamics. Two examples of groups with which I have been associated are illustrative of the presence of group stages:

Case Example 1

One group with whom I introduced the story-linking process was an intergenerational church school class. They had been meeting prior to my joining them and had developed an attentive but passive style of participation. In the beginning, it was clear that they took a somewhat wait-and-see stance. At times, a group member would firmly suggest that we might want to go in another direction from the one toward which we had begun. However, as we continued our weekly sessions, the group members became more and more centered on connecting their situations with the stories in the story-linking process. The group members became increasingly active in the process. Self-disclosures in both the whole group and in small groups gradually came forth freely from nearly every group member. Group members encouraged and supported one another in their sharing and in their choice to be silent. Each person felt free to get his or her point across. Getting to this point did not happen quickly. It happened over time. The number of group members also grew.

Case Example 2

I had been the leader of one group over a short period of time. When we entered into the story-linking process, the group had already moved through a testing period where some group members tended to dominate group discussion. With the beginning of story-linking, they quickly established a mutually oriented rapport. In the beginning, small group members readily pressed capable leaders into service. But, over time, leadership began to rotate. Those who tended to be quiet blossomed in small groups. This gave them courage to share in the whole group setting. There were, in fact, some surprises as persons thought to be very quiet shared their stories in great detail. The group's functioning became that of support group. In some instances, one might say that they got carried away with the process and did not want to stop at certain points in the process. They hoped the group would always continue as it was.

We will explore the dynamics encountered in the developmental stages of groups and how these dynamics are represented in the case examples. We will also explore ways of mediating group processes in light of the stages.

Group Processes During Orientation or Encounter

During the stage of orientation or encounter, group members are uncertain and can be reluctant to share openly. They are concerned about inclusion, acceptance, and solidarity. They also desire clear leadership that is nonthreatening. In Case Example 1, this stage was represented in the group's wait-and-see stance. The first stage was not demonstrably present in Case Example 2 because it had occurred prior to their entry into the story-linking process. Groups at this stage can benefit greatly from the kinds of approaches to convening groups presented earlier. But it is important for leaders/teachers not to compel persons to share. Group members must be allowed freedom to build a personal sense of comfortableness with personal story disclosure within the group setting. If group members respond with reluctance or silence to leader/teacher invitations to whole group sharing, the leader/teacher may move to partner or small group sharing. Sharing in this way can be far less threatening than sharing in a whole group.

Leaders/teachers may also note group members who have difficulty speaking spontaneously. In situations where this kind of difficulty arises, the use of partners or small groups is also warranted. Moreover, if partners or small groups are asked to report back to the whole group, they may be invited before they report to record what they will say on paper or newsprint.

Group Processes During Conflict, Dominance, and Differentiation

Groups move with varying degrees of rapidity into a stage characterized by conflict, dominance, and differentiation. Evidence of a group's movement into this stage can be noted by struggles of group members to reach consensus, dominance of some group members over others, and increased desire among group members to identify the direction the group should go. In Case Example 1, a group member firmly suggested that we might want to go in another direction. In Case 2, the group tested the leadership prior to entering the story-linking process.

Leaders/teachers who recognize the second stage as a normal development of group dynamics are better able to mediate group processes. As groups move into this stage, it is helpful to use the technique of brainstorming. In story-linking, this technique is helpful where group reflection on everyday stories, Bible texts, the faith heritage stories, and Christian decision making are requested. Whether in whole groups or small groups, brainstorming entails first the gathering of ideas without comment. Group discussion and evaluative statements follow.

A second technique in this stage is to pose scenarios such as "If you were to respond to the meaning of this everyday story (or Bible text, or heritage story), what would you say?" Or, "If you were to decide to take personal or group action in response to the story-linking we have done, what would you do?" This technique gives opportunity for individual responses to emerge and to be pooled together. Whole groups, partners, or small groups can then be invited to enter discussion on how to go about prioritizing the responses.

An additional technique that is useful in this stage is role-playing. When there are repeated opportunities to role-play, group members are afforded opportunities to exchange what may be perceived as leading and supportive roles. This is also a way of allowing leadership to emerge from within the group in a rather controlled fashion.

The role of leaders/teachers is not a passive one. Indeed, it is important that leaders/teachers take on a process-observer role in which they observe carefully the behavior of group members and help to facilitate the process of working sensitively together.

Group Processes During Group Cohesiveness and Productivity

The stage of cohesiveness and group productivity is characterized by mutual functioning. Persons are at ease in self-disclosing, and they move through story-linking in a free and relaxed manner. Persons are comfortable with both the group and the story-linking process. In Case Example 1, the group members became increasingly active in the process, free in their self-disclosure and encouraging and supportive of one another. In Case Example 2, the group members quickly established a mutually oriented process.

In this stage, the mutual sojourner role of the leader/teacher and group members can be fully exercised. Even though participants look to the leader/teacher as the one ultimately responsible for group processes, they are able to see the leader/teacher as partner in the story-linking process. This assumes, however, that the leader/teacher has been and continues to be a welcoming presence and an active, sensitive, and disclosive partici-pant throughout the process.

Group Processes During Constructive Independence and Interdependence

In the stage characterized by constructive independence and interde-pendence, the participants are fully invested in their own and others' dis-cerning about what the story-linking process has to say to them. They develop a group consciousness and a consciousness of their belonging in the group. Persons express their interest in the group's continuing to meet and in their own continued engagement in the story-linking process. In Case Example 1, this stage was evidenced in working group relationships that allowed each person to get their point across. In Case Example 2, individuals shared within a support group atmosphere, and they did not want the group to end.

This last developmental stage of group process is both rewarding and challenging. It is rewarding because of the excitement and meaning that are generated in groups at this stage. But a challenge can emerge when groups exhibit ingrown and exclusive tendencies. These tendencies become evident when groups show contentment only with what takes place in the group. They may show inhospitable attitudes toward new group members. There may be limited follow-through on decisions for action made by group members in phase four of the story-linking process. Group members may also seek to lengthen previously agreed upon meet-ing times beyond what is actually feasible or comfortable. When groups exhibit these tendencies, they move away from liberating and vocation-focused dynamics. The role of the leader/teacher is to identify any ten-dencies toward ingrown group dynamics and to reorient the group toward more liberating and vocation-centered ends.

Leaders/teachers may approach this situation by naming what is taking place without placing blame on others and by giving direct guidance. We may say, for example, "I feel uneasy about the direction in which we seem to be going. I would like for us to direct our attention to a timeline for carrying out the decisions we make in our story-linking today and commit to a report on them at the end of the timeline." Similarly, we may guide groups to look at how they may develop welcoming strategies for newcomers and address the length of story-linking sessions. Additional attention will be given to group membership and size as well as time management in the following sections.

Reflection Exercise

Review the stages of group process. Recall any experiences you have had of proceeding through these stages either as a group participant or a group leader.

Tending to Group Membership and Size

It is important to give some attention to group membership and size because each exerts some influence on group processes and dynamics. We will give particular attention to the impact of intergenerational group membership on group dynamics and processes in story-linking. We will also explore ways of mediating intergenerational groups.

Group Membership

In many instances today, relating across the generations is problematic. Single adults, married adults, and youth confront challenges to positive interaction with one another. Involvement of children and senior adults in conversation together with other ages/stages happens with varying degrees of success. Most often, age/stage groupings prevail. And, of course, story-linking may be undertaken by particular age/stage groups, using the approaches described above. However, *Soul Stories* highlights stories emerging within and beyond family and extended family contexts. For this reason, story-linking is highlighted here as a process for intergenerational participation in church, community, home, and retreat settings.

"Intergenerational participation" refers to the communal engagement in story-linking through face-to-face sharing of persons from two or more generations or life stages (senior adults, middle-aged adults, young adults, youths, and children). Through intergenerational group membership, we seek to create communal-oriented group dynamics. We promote these dynamics when we foster appreciation for one another's uniqueness. We also promote these dynamics when we acknowledge the contribution each person from the various generations can make to story-linking, to one another's formation of liberating wisdom, and to one another's liberation and hope-filled vocation.

However, accomplishing this requires that we understand generational differences, conflicts, and difficulties in intergenerational group interaction.

Generational Differences

African Americans bring to story-linking the experiences and behaviors associated with their particular life stages. African Americans from each life stage also bring personal values and views informed by the specific era in which they were born and reared. These stage-specific factors produce generational differences.

Generational differences can cause conflict or create resistance when persons criticize, confront, blame, or reject one another. This kind of conflict can either discourage intergenerational participation or create a restrictive atmosphere. Moreover, group members may not understand the benefit of positive or creative conflict in which persons encourage one another to share their perspectives and strive to hear and respond in respectful ways to different perspectives.

Persons may also have difficulty entering into intergenerational participation in story-linking because they are unaccustomed to this kind of participation in Christian education. For some, this kind of difficulty may derive from customary participation in stage-based or age-based Christian education experiences. The question is: How do we mediate group processes, given these several types of dynamics?

Mediating Intergenerational Group Processes

Prior to entering into story-linking with an intergenerational group, it is important that leaders confirm within themselves the value of such a group. Leaders must feel secure in their own life stage and uniqueness and their ability to affirm the value and uniqueness of others. They should ask themselves these questions:

- Do I affirm the right and the need of African Americans from the various life stages to share their perspectives?
- Am I willing to invest deeply in a loving and caring group process?
- Do I recognize my own limitations and biases?
- Am I willing to continually tend to the sensitivities of others?

How leaders/teachers function in the actual intergenerational group setting is pivotal to how persons from differing generations relate to one another. When we function as mutual sojourners in the story-linking process and are relaxed and open, we encourage the same functioning in group members. We show ourselves as mutual sojourners in the intergenerational setting when we self-disclose willingly, freely express affirming caring feelings, maintain eye contact with others who are talking, and listen attentively so that others can accept responsibility for speaking.

Leaders/teachers are also responsible for involving the intergenerational group in the actual story-linking process in positive ways. I have found three approaches helpful.

First, create nonthreatening opportunities for persons to share their thoughts, ideas, and insights. This may be promoted by asking indirect questions, particularly in the beginning of the story-linking process. To do this, we invite persons to "talk through" the actors in case studies, Bible stories/texts, and African American faith heritage stories. For example, we may ask: "Who in the stories are of greatest interest to you, and why? Who were of least interest and why? In what ways do you think the stories tell about things that happen today?" As persons become more comfortable in responding to indirect questions, we may move to more direct questions such as: "In what ways do you see yourself in the stories? How do the stories speak to you in your situation?"

Second, persons of every life stage tend to respond actively to role-playing, dramatizations, and singing and can, therefore, be readily integrated into these activities. It is especially helpful to use role-playing or dramatizations where everyone has a part or that are easily repeated so that parts may be rotated.

In using songs, however, it is important to be sensitive to the differing musical tastes of persons in the various stages. It is helpful to give a forthright invitation to group members to choose, sing, and even teach one another to intone their favorite spirituals, gospel songs, rap music, or hymns. Such an invitation communicates the leader's/teacher's understanding of the enrichment derived from intergenerational sharing of music.

Third, we may promote positive intergenerational participation by using small groups during response and reflection periods in the story-linking process. Leaders/teachers should not hesitate to invite small groups to consider how they can encourage the active participation of all members. To do this, leaders/teachers set as expectations the group members' attentive and respectful response to one another. We may ask small group members to seek a consensus on ground rules regarding rotation of small leaders, recorders, and spokespersons for the group.

Where children are present, small group members may integrate them into the group by retelling stories used in story-linking in shortened, condensed form and in ways that emphasize the role of children in the stories. They may then ask a child to tell the stories in the child's own words. The small group then undertakes a discussion about the meaning of the stories and includes the children in the discussion.

Reflection Exercise

Envision how you would mediate in positive ways an intergenerational group comprised of adults, youths, and children.

Group Size

The size of a group will have some bearing on group processes and dynamics. The story-linking process is suitable for as few as two persons. In this case, there is no leader/teacher. The two persons merely engage in a mutual dialogue and reflection following the phases of the story-linking process. When various sizes of family groupings, church school groups, retreat, or other groups engage in story-linking, the designated leader/teacher mediates the group process according to the information provided above. Generally, active group participation can be attained more easily in small groups of around ten to twelve persons. In larger groups, it is helpful to utilize partners and small groups of three or four persons who can provide a sense of closeness and intimacy in dialogue and reflection.

Reflection Exercise

Envision how you would engage in the story-linking process with one other person who is younger or older than yourself. Then envision how you would lead either a small group of four to five family members, or another group of ten or more persons in story-linking.

Time Management

Each story-linking session is designed to take about one and one-half hours. If time does not permit completion of the process in a single session and several days will elapse before your next time together, the process is best undertaken in segments. When it is segmented, phases one and two may be completed in one session. Phases three and four may be completed in a successive session. Dividing story-linking in this way allows for more cohesive movement through the process.

Decisions on when to undertake the whole process or part of it depend on the time frame made available. For example, one-hour time frames for church school settings would necessitate dividing the process as noted above. The segmented process might also be considered for a series of weeknight or Saturday sessions, or for periodic partner or family sessions. Weekend retreat settings typically allow for a series of sessions with relatively short break times in between sessions. Therefore, in such settings, each phase of the story-linking process may be engaged singly.

When the intergenerational participants in story-linking are assembled, attention needs to be given to timing the movement through the process. This kind of time management entails paying careful attention to skillful, yet timely, guidance of participants through every step of the process.

Leaders/teachers may aid group processes by stating up front the time frame allotted for each step of the story-linking process. However, in moving through each step, it is important that leaders/teachers be guided by an internal sense of timing. Knowing when to bring closure to group dialogue and reflection and when dialogue should continue is both a gift and a skill that leaders/teachers will develop over time.

Being attuned to what we hear, see, and feel as leaders/teachers during the group's activities will guide our sense of timing. For example, being attuned means noticing when spontaneous exuberant dialogue has moved beyond its peak and the time has come to move on. It also means noticing when lengthy dialogue and reflection, even though intense, must be brought to a close for the sake of moving on to another step and a deeper level of insight and understanding. Such an awareness may prompt the leader/teacher to affirm the group's active participation, indicate the need to move on in the interest of time, and seek the group's agreement to do so. Being attuned may also mean sensing from a participant's expectant or troubled look, forward sitting stance, or half-raised hand that time is needed to encourage and hear her or his response.

In short, knowing the right time to move on to the next step is not an exact science. It is a creative spiritual awareness. It is being in touch with God's moment of bringing meaning to a group or members within it. We call this being in touch with *kairos*, or God's significant moment of acting in our lives.

Reflection Exercise

What decisions about time management would you make in regard to story-linking? On what basis would you decide?

Constructing an Inviting Physical Setting

The arrangement of the physical setting can have a positive or negative effect on group processes. Consequently, attention should be given to it. Of particular importance are such matters as lighting and seating that respond appropriately to the various age-groups that will be involved. Moreover, optimal participation occurs when group members are seated in a circle arrangement rather than in theater rows where they cannot have face-to-face contact. Where possible, rooms should also be chosen that allow for movement of chairs into small groups or for role-playing and dramatizations.

When using tape recorders to disclose stories in the story-linking process, it is necessary to assure a volume level that is adequate for the room size and the hearing needs of group members. Materials such as Bibles, PowerPoint equipment and supports, newsprint, markers, tape, writing or drawing paper, pencils, pens, crayons, or other desired supplies should be placed on a list and brought in before the group's arrival in the meeting room.

Reflection Exercise

Consider a physical setting for undertaking the story-linking process. Where is this setting? What seating and equipment are already there?

What arrangements would you need to make in order to create an inviting and comfortable physical setting?

Caring for Those Who Struggle with Their Stories

Recalling our stories as we see them in someone else's story or in the throes of telling them can evoke deep emotion. These experiences of deep emotion sometimes give way to sighing, crying, or other expressions accompanying the recall of painful memories. In this situation, the leader/teacher may become a gentle, silent presence beside the person as the group continues its activities. The teacher/leader may also ask the person if there is assistance that would be helpful. The person may simply indicate that she/he is all right and that no assistance is needed. In other cases, especially when the show of emotion is intense or does not abate, it may seem appropriate for group members to be guided by the teacher/leader or to move spontaneously to attend to the person experiencing painful memories. Attending involves a wide range of responses. Responses may include simply being present to the person, or touching or laying on of hands when there is a sense of its appropriateness, or inviting her/him to tell what would be helpful, or offering prayers of intercession if requested.

We cannot always assume that a show of emotion results from feelings of pain or sadness. There are times when remembering brings joy that moves persons to tears or other expressions of emotion. Yet, we cannot know unless we seek answers from persons to the questions: "Are you all right? May we help you in any way?" The important point here is that tending to persons during their moments of deep emotion is necessary, and doing so is part of modeling the meaning of an emancipatory environment for story-linking.

Encouraging Follow-Up

Follow-up takes the form not simply of assuring movement through the phases of the story-linking process within an established Christian education setting, but of suggesting and anticipating uses of story-linking beyond that specific context. In light of the quest of persons today for up-close, face-to-face relationships in their homes and community settings, leaders/teachers may encourage participants to engage in story-linking to build these relationships in agreed upon family times, with friends, or other designated groupings. Teachers/leaders of established Christian education settings of their congregations may also explore uses of story-linking in settings often left out as valid and important Christian education contexts. Over the years, I and students of mine have included in these contexts senior adult centers and living environments, shelters for homeless individuals and families, and prisons.

Reflection Exercise

Consider a physical setting for undertaking the story-linking process. Where is this setting? What seating and equipment are already there? What arrangements would you need to make in order to create an inviting and comfortable physical setting?

In this chapter, I have introduced approaches to group dynamics and processes in carrying out the story-linking model. My intent has been to suggest approaches to convening groups, mediating groups based on an understanding of developmental stages of groups, tending to group membership and size, time management, and constructing inviting physical settings. The approaches came out of my own experiences. I hope leaders, teachers, and others involved in story-linking will modify them to suit their own specific settings.

NOTES

Preface

1. See Anne E. Streaty Wimberly and Evelyn L. Parker, *In Search of Wisdom: Faith Formation in the Black Church* (Nashville: Abingdon Press, 2002).

2. Cornel West, *Race Matters* (New York: Vintage Books, 1994), pp. 9-10, 19. Also see Robert Staples and Leanor Boulin Johnson, *Black Families at the Crossroads: Challenges and Prospects* (San Francisco: Jossey-Bass, 1993), pp. 240-41. It is important to insert here that the situation of African American families today is not necessarily unique to them. Balswick and Balswick state unequivocally that "one of the major themes in modern society is individualism. Individualism has caused us to focus on the individual's needs and perspective rather than on relationships and groups. When analyzing contemporary society, we see the delicate balance between individual rights and family rights has been skewed in favor of individual rights." See Jack O. Balswick and Judith K. Balswick, *The Family: A Christian Perspective on the Contemporary Home*, 2nd ed. (Grand Rapids: Baker Books, 1999), pp. 37-38.

3. The black church has traditionally served as extended family. Yet, there is renewed need for it to be the place where the stories of families are welcomed, shared, and informed by the belief system and values that counter those in society that frustrate a sense of liberation and vocation. A similar view of the role of the church appears in: Balswick and Balswick, *The Family: A Christian Perspective on the Contemporary Home*, pp. 355-56.

Prologue

1. Hewlett and West describe the current situation in terms of "the depletion of our social capital—that store of trust, connectedness, and engagement in community life." They go on to say that the sense of belonging and oral anchoring is under siege in current-day families, neighborhoods, schools, congregations, and other institutions. See Sylvia Ann Hewlett and Cornel West, *The War Against Parents* (Boston: Houghton Mifflin Company, 1998), p. 51.

2. These comments emerging in conversation about the relevance and future of Christian education confirm my own concerns about the impact of technological development and, most particularly, cyberspace, on face-to-face communal relationships. See: Anne Streaty Wimberly, "The Faith Community as Listener in the Era of Cyberspace,"

and "In Search of the Listener: Receptivity, Bearing Witness, and Formation of Self in the Era of Cyberspace," *Journal of the Interdenominational Theological Center* 25(2), Fall 1997:13-40.

3. See Anne Streaty Wimberly, "The Faith Community as Listener in the Era of Cyberspace," pp. 41-42. Michael Nichols also warns that when inadequate attention and understanding are given, persons become insecure in themselves and less open to others. He also reminds us that "the listening we don't get is the listening we don't pass on." See Michael Nichol, *The Lost Art of Listening* (New York: Guilford Press, 1995), p. 248.

4. Cornel West writes about the availability of cultural resources in the past. But he comes to a divergent point of view on people's responses to the current absence of these resources. He has observed a disturbing passivity among people that he contends feeds people's sense of meaninglessness, lovelessness, and hopelessness. See Cornel West, *The Cornel West Reader* (New York: Basic Civitas Books, 1999), p. 293.

5. See Stephen Crites, "The Narrative Quality of Experience," *Journal of the American Academy of Religion* 39(3), September 1971:291.

6. Theodore R. Sarbin, "The Narrative as a Root Metaphor for Psychology," in *Narrative Psychology: The Storied Nature of Human Conduct,* ed. Theodore R. Sarbin (New York: Praeger Publishers, 1986), p. 4.

7. Donald Capps, *Reframing: A Method in Pastoral Care* (Minneapolis: Fortress Press, 1990), p. 139.

8. Andrew D. Lester, *Hope in Pastoral Care and Counseling* (Louisville: Westminster John Knox Press, 1995), p. 139.

9. See Thomas H. Groome, *Sharing Faith: A Comprehensive Approach to Religious Education and Pastoral Ministry—The Way of Shared Praxis* (San Francisco: HarperSanFrancisco, 1991), p. 109; Jerry H. Stone, "Narrative Theology and Religious Education," in *Theologies of Religious Education,* ed. Randolph Crump Miller (Birmingham: Religious Education Press, 1995), p. 255.

10. Jerry Stone, "Narrative Theology and Religious Education," pp. 255, 262-64, 268.

11. Gilmour emphasizes that reading and writing our stories or memoirs enable us to see God at work in our lives. His book actually presents a model for reading and writing them. See Peter Gilmour, *The Wisdom of Memoir: Reading and Writing Life's Sacred Texts* (Winona, MN: St. Mary's Press, 1997).

12. Anne Streaty Wimberly, *Soul Stories: African American Christian Education,* 1st ed. (Nashville: Abingdon Press, 1994), p. 38; Andrew Lester, *Hope in Pastoral Care and Counseling,* p. 33.

13. See Robert Alter, *The Art of Biblical Narrative* (New York: Basic Books, 1981); Stanley Hauerwas, *A Community of Character* (Notre Dame, IN: University of Notre Dame Press, 1981), pp. 36-52.

14. Anne E. Streaty Wimberly, "A Legacy of Hope: African-American Christian Education During the Era of Slavery," *Journal of the Interdenominational Theological Center* 23(2), Spring 1996:3-23 (8-17).

15. A full discussion of the history and major motifs of black theology appears in Gayraud S. Wilmore, *Pragmatic Spirituality: The Christian Faith Through an Africentric Lens* (New York: New York University Press, 2004), pp. 155-66. See also Cornel West, *The Cornel West Reader,* pp. 393-94.

16. Wilmore describes the struggle, in fact, as "indigenous to the fallen world, the sinful environment in which we all must live," which every generation must continue to

work to confront or "to rebuild the terraces of realism and hope . . . to tidy up the world of interracial and interethnic relations in faithfulness and obedience to Christ." See Wilmore, *Pragmatic Theology*, p. 277.

17. See West, *The Cornel West Reader*, p. 394.

18. Anne E. Streaty Wimberly and Evelyn L. Parker, *In Search of Wisdom: Faith Formation in the Black Church* (Nashville: Abingdon Press, 2002), pp. 13, 16.

19. This understanding of liberating wisdom is a paraphrase of the words from J. Glenn Gray, *The Promise of Wisdom: An Introduction to Philosophy of Education* (Philadelphia: Lippincott Company, 1968), p. 21.

20. Andrew Billingsley, *Mighty Like a River: The Black Church and Social Reform* (New York: Oxford University Press, 1999).

21. Frederick Douglass, *Narrative of the Life of Frederick Douglass, An American Slave* (New York: Signet Books, 1968), p. 103.

22. Douglass, *Narrative of the Life of Frederick Douglass*, p. 108.

23. Ibid., p. 117.

24. Ibid., p. 90.

1. A Story-Linking Process

1. The song "The Lord Is My Light" appears in the *African American Heritage Hymnal* (Chicago: GIA Publications, Inc., 2001), no. 160.

2. The song "I Don't Feel No Ways Tired" appears in the *African American Heritage Hymnal*, no. 414.

3. An analogous use of Bible stories is cited by Edward P. Wimberly in what he refers to as "a biblical narrative model for pastoral counseling." In that model, the Bible becomes a part of the counseling process of persons who are from Bible-rich traditions. The growth-facilitative-authoritative use of Bible is seen as a way of engendering persons' discernment process and their self-growth. See Edward P. Wimberly, *Using Scripture in Pastoral Counseling* (Nashville: Abingdon Press, 1994), pp. 10, 14.

4. See Dorothee Soelle, *Death By Bread Alone: Texts and Reflections on Religious Experience* (Philadelphia: Fortress Press, 1978), pp. 121-23; Walter Brueggemann, *The Message of the Psalms* (Minneapolis: Augsburg Press, 1984), p. 26.

2. Exploring Self and World Through Story-Linking

1. See J. Clinton McCann Jr., "The Book of Psalms: Introduction, Commentary, and Reflections," in *The New Interpreter's Bible*, vol. 4 (Nashville: Abingdon Press, 1996), pp. 1235, 1237.

2. See Dorothee Soelle, *Death by Bread Alone: Texts and Reflections on Religious Experience* (Philadelphia: Fortress Press, 1978), pp. 121-23; Walter Brueggemann, *The Message of the Psalms* (Minneapolis: Augsburg Press, 1984), p. 26.

3. See Dorothy Soelle, *Death by Bread Alone*, p. 122.

4. Howard Thurman, *Jesus and the Disinherited* (Richmond, IN: Friends United Press, 1981), p. 50.

5. Dyson makes the point that there are multiple meanings to any given text and that "language itself is a metaphor for the extraordinary elasticity of human identity. Race only

compounds the metaphor's complexity." We see an application of this view, when he later says that "observers and critics outside hip-hop culture often miss the war being waged within its borders because they ignore its different forms, shapes, and textures. . . . [T]hey don't necessarily embody the stigma that dogs them." See Michael Eric Dyson, *Open Mike: Reflections on Philosophy, Race, Sex, Culture and Religion* (New York: Basic *Civitas* Books, 2003), pp. 50-51, 294-95.

6. The song appears in *Lift Every Voice and Sing II: An African American Hymnal* (New York: The Church Hymnal Corporation, 1993), no. 16.

7. The spiritual is found in *Songs of Zion: Supplemental Worship Resources 12* (Nashville: Abingdon Press, 1981), no. 132.

3. Exploring Relationships and Events of Our Lives Through Story-Linking

1. A helpful guide to the story appears in Robert W. Wall, "The Acts of the Apostles: Introduction, Commentary, and Reflections," in *The New Interpreter's Bible*. vol. 10 (Nashville: Abingdon Press, 2002), pp. 344–53.

2. The story here is excerpted and largely paraphrased from Josiah Henson, *Father Henson's Story of His Own Life* (Boston: John P. Jewett and Company, 1858).

3. See Jessie Carney Smith, ed., "Irene McCoy Gaines," *Notable Black American Women* (Detroit: Gale Research, Inc., 1992), pp. 383-86.

4. See H. Beecher Hicks Jr., *Preaching Through the Storm* (Grand Rapids, MI: Ministry Resources, 1987), pp. 21-34.

5. A version of the song is found in the *African American Heritage Hymnal* (Chicago: GIA Publications, Inc., 2001), no. 414.

6. A version of the song is found in *Lift Every Voice and Sing II: An African American Hymnal* (New York: The Church Hymnal Corporation, 1993), no. 200.

4. Exploring Life Meanings Through Story-Linking

1. In planning for the use of the scriptural passages in Hebrews, the following materials are helpful: Fred Craddock, "The Letter to the Hebrews: Introduction, Commentary, and Reflections," *The New Interpreter's Bible*, vol. 12 (Nashville: Abingdon Press, 1998), pp. 3-24, 124-49; Robert Jewett, *Letter to Pilgrims* (New York: Pilgrim Press, 1981).

2. A version of the song also entitled "I Don't Feel No Ways Tired" appears in the *African American Heritage Hymnal* (Chicago: GIA Publications, Inc., 2001), no. 414.

3. The first-person depictions are built on information appearing in Paul J. Achtemeier, *Harper's Bible Dictionary* (San Francisco: Harper & Row, 1985).

4. Frederick Douglass, *Narrative of the Life of Frederick Douglass: An American Slave* (New York: Signet Books, 1968), pp. 76-77.

5. Ibid., p. 83.

6. Ibid., p. 111.

7. Sarah Bradford, *Harriet Tubman: The Moses of Her People* (New York: Corinth, 1961), p. 31.

8. M. W. Taylor, *Harriet Tubman* (New York: Chelsea House, 1991), p. 39.

9. Ibid., p. 73.

10. Ibid., pp. 50-51.

11. This gospel song is found in the *African American Heritage Hymnal*, no. 333.

12. This spiritual in found in the *African American Heritage Hymnal*, no. 391.

13. This spiritual is found in the *African American Heritage Hymnal*, no. 541.

14. This spiritual is found in the *African American Heritage Hymnal*, no. 524.

15. See Langston Hughes, "Mother to Son," in *Children of Promise. African-American Literature and Art for Young People*, ed. Charles Sullivan (New York: Harry N. Abrams, 1991), p. 67.

5. The Pivotal Role of Scripture in Story-Linking and How to Choose Scripture

1. A traditional version and a contemporary arrangement of the spiritual are found in *Songs of Zion* (Nashville: Abingdon Press, 1981), no. 112 and no. 212.

2. See William M. Philpot, ed., *Best Black Sermons* (Valley Forge: Judson Press, 1972), pp. 25-30.

3. See Lance Watson, "That Was Then, This Is Now: A Message for Pastors," *African American Pulpit* 6(1), Winter 2002–2003:75-78.

4. The spiritual is found in *Songs of Zion*, no. 106.

5. The spiritual is found in *Songs of Zion*, no. 94.

6. Samuel D. Proctor and William D. Watley, *Sermons From the Black Pulpit* (Valley Forge: Judson Press, 1984), pp. 107-13.

7. See Jeremiah A. Wright, "Faith Under Fire," *African American Pulpit* 5(2), Spring 2002:96-100.

8. The spiritual is found in *Lift Every Voice and Sing II: An African American Hymnal* (New York: The Church Hymnal Corporation, 1993), no. 169.

9. Sojourner Truth tells her mother's frequent use of the language of the psalmist. See Margaret Washington, ed., *Narrative of Sojourner Truth* (New York: Vintage Books, 1933), p. 7.

10. This was a phrase that Josiah Henson heard his mother cry out on an occasion when her children were sold away from her one by one. See Josiah Henson, *Father Henson's Story of His Own Life* (Boston: John P. Jewett and Company, 1858), pp. 12-13.

11. This prayer song is found in *Lift Every Voice and Sing II*, no. 162.

12. This prayer song is found in *Lift Every Voice and Sing II*, no. 166.

13. A version of the spiritual is found in *Songs of Zion*, no. 123.

14. The song is found in the *African American Heritage Hymnal* (Chicago: GIA Publications, Inc., 2001), no. 497.

15. See Clay Evans, "The Lord Is My Shepherd," *African American Pulpit* 5(3), Summer 2002:50-53.

16. This hymn is found in *Songs of Zion*, no. 14.

17. This gospel hymn is found in the *African American Heritage Hymnal*, no. 160.

18. The spiritual is found in *Songs of Zion*, no. 85.

19. The spiritual is found in the *African American Heritage Hymnal*, no. 541.

20. This sermon appears in Samuel D. Proctor and William D. Watley, *Sermons from the Black Pulpit* (Valley Forge: Judson Press, 1984), pp. 99-106.

21. The gospel hymn is found in the *African American Heritage Hymnal*, no. 404.

22. See Linda Gobodo, "The Power of a Purpose," *African American Pulpit* 4(4), Fall 2001:49-53.

23. See James Weldon Johnson and J. Rosamund Johnson, *The Books of American Negro Spirituals*, vol. 1 (New York: Viking Press, 1964), pp. 96-98.

24. This traditional African-American song is found in the *African American Heritage Hymnal*, no. 222.

25. The song is found in the *African American Heritage Hymnal*, no. 549.

26. The spiritual is found in *Lift Every Voice and Sing II*, no. 148.

27. The gospel hymn by Charles A. Tindley is found in *Lift Every Voice and Sing II*, no. 200.

28. The spiritual is found in the *African American Heritage Hymnal*, no. 349.

29. The gospel anthem by Mary A. Baker is found in the *African American Heritage Hymnal*, no. 221.

30. The gospel song by Rev. Maceo Woods appears in the *African American Heritage Hymnal*, no. 407.

31. The gospel song written by George D. Elderkin is found in *The New Baptist Hymnal*, 6th ed. (Nashville: National Baptist Publishing Board, 1980), no. 514.

32. The gospel hymn by Civilla D. Martin appears in *Songs of Zion*, no. 33, and in the *African American Heritage Hymnal*, no. 143.

33. The spiritual is found in James Weldon Johnson and J. Rosamund Johnson, *The Books of American Negro Spirituals*, vol. 2, pp. 155-57.

34. This traditional African American song is found in the *African American Heritage Hymnal*, no. 238.

35. The song is found in the *African American Heritage Hymnal*, no. 249.

36. The gospel song by V. Michael McKay is found in the *African American Heritage Hymnal*, no. 179.

37. The gospel song by Kenneth W. Louis appears in the *African American Heritage Hymnal*, no. 231.

38. The spiritual appears in *Lift Every Voice and Sing II*, no. 33.

39. The spiritual appears in the *African American Heritage Hymnal*, no. 686, and in *Songs of Zion*, no. 88.

40. Even though the hymn emerged outside the African American context, it is revered by African Americans and is sung in a unique African American improvisational style. The hymn appears in the *African American Heritage Hymnal*, nos. 271, 272.

41. The gospel song by Franklin D. Williams appears in the *African American Heritage Hymnal*, no. 270.

42. The song is found in the *African American Heritage Hymnal*, no. 434, and in *Songs of Zion*, no. 235.

43. See Walter H. Brooks, *The Pastor's Voice* (Washington, DC: Associated Publishers, 1945), p. 113.

44. The spiritual is found in the *African American Heritage Hymnal*, no. 463, and in *Songs of Zion*, no. 76.

45. The spiritual is found in the *African American Heritage Hymnal*, no. 541.

46. The gospel song by Margaret Pleasant Douroux appears in the *African American Heritage Hymnal*, no. 461.

47. The spiritual appears in the *African American Heritage Hymnal*, no. 131.

48. The spiritual appears in the *African American Heritage Hymnal*, no. 391.

49. The gospel song by Albert Goodson is found in the *African American Heritage Hymnal*, no. 412.

50. The gospel song by Curtis Burrell appears in the *African American Heritage Hymnal*, no. 414.

51. For the precise method presented by Hessel, see Dieter T. Hessel, "Developing a Whole Parish Praxis," pp. 269-72 in *Social Themes of the Christian Year* (Louisville: Westminster/John Knox Press, 1983). The seven points can be found on pp. 270-72.

BIBLIOGRAPHY

Alter, Robert. *The Art of Biblical Narrative*. New York: Basic Books, 1981.

Balswick, Jack O., and Judith K. Balswick. *The Family: A Christian Perspective on the Contemporary Home*. 2nd ed. Grand Rapids: Baker Books, 1999.

Billingsley, Andrew. *Mighty Like A River: The Black Church and Social Reform*. New York: Oxford University Press, 1999.

Bradford, Sarah. *Harriet Tubman: The Moses of Her People*. New York: Corinth, 1961.

Brueggemann, Walter. *The Message of the Psalms*. Minneapolis: Augsburg Press, 1984.

Capps, Donald. *Reframing: A Method in Pastoral Care*. Minneapolis: Fortress Press, 1990.

Craddock, Fred. "The Letter to the Hebrews: Introduction, Commentary, and Reflections." In *The New Interpreter's Bible*. Vol. 12. Nashville: Abingdon Press, 1998.

Crites, Stephen. "The Narrative Quality of Experience." *Journal of the American Academy of Religion*, 39(3), September 1971:291.

Douglass, Frederick. *Narrative of the Life of Frederick Douglass, An American Slave*. New York: Signet Books, 1968.

Dyson, Michael Eric. *Open Mike: Reflections on Philosophy, Race, Sex, Culture and Religion*. New York: Basic Civitas Books, 2003.

Evans, Clay. "The Lord Is My Shepherd." *African American Pulpit* 5(3), Summer 2002:50-53.

Gilmour, Peter. *The Wisdom of Memoir: Reading and Writing Life's Sacred Texts*. Winona, MN: St. Mary's Press, 1997.

Gobodo, Linda. "The Power of a Purpose." *African American Pulpit* 4(4), Fall 2001:49-53.

Gray, J. Glenn. *The Promise of Wisdom: An Introduction to Philosophy of Education*. Philadelphia: Lippincott Company, 1968.

Groome, Thomas H. *Sharing Faith: A Comprehensive Approach to Religious Education and Pastoral Ministry—The Way of Shared Praxis*. San Francisco: HarperSanFrancisco, 1991.

Henson, Josiah. *Father Henson's Story of His Own Life*. Boston: John P. Jewett and Company, 1858.

Hessel, Dieter T. "Developing a Whole Parish Praxis." In *Social Themes of the Christian Year*. Louisville: Westminster/John Knox Press, 1983.

Hewlett, Sylvia, and Cornel West. *The War Against Parents*. Boston: Houghton Mifflin Company, 1998.

Hicks, H. Beecher Jr. *Preaching Through the Storm*. Grand Rapids: Ministry Resources, 1987.

Hughes, Langston. "Mother to Son." In *Children of Promise: African American Literature and Art for Young People*, edited by Charles Sullivan. New York: Harry N. Abrams, 1991.

Jewett, Robert. *Letter to Pilgrims*. New York: Pilgrim Press, 1981.

Johnson, James Weldon, and J. Rosamund Johnson. *The Books of American Negro Spirituals*, Vols. 1 and 2. New York: Viking Press, 1964.

Lester, Andrew D. *Hope in Pastoral Care and Counseling*. Louisville: Westminster John Knox Press, 1995.

McCann, J. Clinton Jr. "The Book of Psalms: Introduction, Commentary, and Reflections." In *The New Interpreter's Bible*. Vol. 4. Nashville: Abingdon Press, 1996.

Nichols, Michael. *The Lost Art of Listening*. New York: Guilford Press, 1995.

Philpot, William M., ed. *Best Black Sermons*. Valley Forge: Judson Press, 1972.

Proctor, Samuel D., and William D. Watley. *Sermons from the Black Pulpit*. Valley Forge: Judson Press, 1984.

Sarbin, Theodore R. "The Narrative as a Root Metaphor for Psychology." In *Narrative Psychology: The Storied Nature of Human Conduct*, edited by Theodore R. Sarbin. New York: Praeger Publishers, 1986.

Smith, Jessie Carney., ed. "Irene McCoy Gaines." In *Notable Black American Women*. Detroit: Gale Research, Inc., 1992.

Soelle, Dorothee. *Death by Bread Alone: Texts and Reflections on Religious Experience*. Philadelphia: Fortress Press, 1978.

Staples, Robert, and Leanor Boulin Johnson. *Black Families at the Crossroads: Challenges and Prospects*. San Francisco: Jossey-Bass, 1993.

Stone, Jerry H. "Narrative Theology and Religious Education." In *Theologies of Religious Education*, edited by Randolph Crump Miller. Birmingham: Religious Education Press, 1995.

Taylor, M. W. *Harriet Tubman*. New York: Chelsea House, 1991.

Thurman, Howard. *Jesus and the Disinherited*. Richmond, IN: Friends United Press, 1981.

Wall, Robert W. "The Acts of the Apostles: Introduction, Commentary, and Reflections." In *The New Interpreter's Bible*. Vol. 10. Nashville: Abingdon Press, 2002.

Washington, Margaret., ed. *Narrative of Sojourner Truth*. New York: Vintage Books, 1933.

Watson, Lance. "That Was Then, This Is Now: A Message for Pastors." *African American Pulpit* 6(1), Winter 2002–2003:75-78.

West, Cornel. *Race Matters*. New York: Vintage Books, 1994.

————. *The Cornel West Reader*. New York: Basic Civitas Books, 1999.

Wilmore, Gayraud S. *Pragmatic Spirituality: The Christian Faith Through an Africentric Lens*. New York: New York University Press, 2004.

Wimberly, Anne Streaty. "A Legacy of Hope: African-American Christian Education During the Era of Slavery." *Journal of the Interdenominational Theological Center* 23(2), Spring 1996:3-23.

————. *Soul Stories: African American Christian Education*. 1st ed. Nashville: Abingdon Press, 1994.

————. "The Faith Community as Listener in the Era of Cyberspace," and "In Search of the Listener: Receptivity, Bearing Witness, and Formation of Self in the Era of Cyberspace." *Journal of the Interdenominational Theological Center* 25(2), Fall 1997:13-40.

Wimberly, Anne E. Streaty, and Evelyn L. Parker. *In Search of Wisdom: Faith Formation in the Black Church*. Nashville: Abingdon Press, 2002.

Wimberly, Edward P. *Using Scripture in Pastoral Counseling*. Nashville: Abingdon Press, 1994.

Wright, Jeremiah A. "Faith Under Fire." *African American Pulpit* 5(2), Spring 2002:96-100.